RENOIR

RENOIR

BY

MICHEL FLORISOONE

TRANSLATED FROM THE FRENCH

BY

GEORGE FREDERIC LEES

WILLIAM HEINEMANN LTD
LONDON   TORONTO

RENOIR

THE XIXth century was a prey to restlessness. It was obsessed with the idea of progress, consumed by superhuman and even inhuman desires, pregnant with many possibilities, swayed between Romanticism and Classicism. As a result it lost contact first with mankind and then with Nature itself, which tended to dematerialize as if at the touch of a magician's wand. In the closing years of this despairing century — incapable, between the trembling movements which characterized its senility, of doing more than include each passing second in its mirages and illusions — Renoir, despite his changes of style, seems to express an untimely sense of continuity. He was as continuous as life itself, which, full of assurance and certain of its destiny, never deviates a hair's breadth from its course and is indifferent to everyday events. He remained unvaryingly wise, modest, discreet, happy to be alive; he revived, amidst days of defeat and decadence, the sweetness of human existence. He enabled that century — torn between the extremes of terror and apathy, between emotional exuberance and spiritual aridity, between the spectres of the guillotine, the barricades and voluptuous frenzy — to know in the end the richest and tenderest of feelings : the love of life.

It was a love so strong that Renoir might have lived in any age whatsoever. The happenings of the moment had no significance for him. Renoir displayed that indifference which children have towards anything that is not of their own invention : their dreams played in grim earnest. This was not innocence on his part, for Renoir was a sinner like other men; and on no account would he make himself conspicuous by any form of abnormal chastity. He had committed the carnal fault as others had done, yet he lived as though that fault had never been consummated, as though sentence for the crime had never been passed. The state of sin being the state of nature, it became in his eyes the primary state, the state of Truth; and since Renoir could conceive only what is, the commonplace became his ideal; what was habitual became identical with what was original. Nothing displays more banality than Renoir's work, but with it is freshness, because to him each day was as it were a first day, and his eye like his sensibility was never the worse for wear. Unknown to him was that failing of a man who begins to be worn out through contact with things and who can no longer admire because habit has blunted both his heart and his feelings. To Renoir everything was an object and a subject of wonder; he recreated in us the very faculty of wonder in the presence of nature, of that commonplace miracle : the world of creation. It was that faculty which enabled him to discover beauty in trivial things and greatness in the little occurrences around him, to see what was rare and precious beneath a vulgar surface. Rules and codes were unnecessary — beauty was to be found wherever there was a product of Nature, above all a manifestation of life. It was visible in what was elementary, in instinct, in fecundity; and Renoir had no need to wave, as though they were protective flags, the names of Paganism or Pantheism, in order to express his wholly simple love of life.

There was nothing savage or primitive about Renoir's painting; nor did he go about it as the bird sings, or as the appletree bears its fruit. His mental outlook remained neither unsophisticated nor stagnant.   Renoir's life — like every life which has been really lived — was a conquest.   A smiling conquest, resembling more a stroll in a fertile garden loaded with beautiful ripe fruit than an exhausting or glorious march across battlefields.   But it was a conquest all the same, — a slow and persevering ascent, comparable to a calm tide slowly encroaching on a sandy beach, — the gradual ascent of one who strove toward a universal understanding of the whole of creation.   By slow degrees, Renoir rose from pleasure to joy, — from the pleasure of living, feeling, tasting, enjoying, loving physically and spontaneously to the joy of possessing, retaining and breathing deeply.   And that more spiritual joy led him to a condition of happy serenity.   There was more beauty and satisfaction in the contemplation of the powerful inner life than in the enjoyment of its seductive effects, which were fleeting and superficial.   More and more strongly was Renoir impressed by the mystery of birth, by the grandeur of the creative act, and by that marvel in the form of a creature which has at last attained the fulness of its maturity.   And from that summit Renoir embraced the whole of creation, condensed it in the human fruit, instinctively understood the unique principle of life and the relations which bind all living things together, discovered the initial identity of matter, and perceived the analogy between all creatures.   At the close of his life, without meditation and perhaps without even realizing the fact, he entered into so intimate a communion with Nature that he could no longer distinguish her; he did not strive, like Cézanne or Van Gogh, to dominate and drag from her some awful secret; becoming absorbed in her, he hid himself — humble and full of adoration — in her very heart.   Himself a creature, he took his rank as one among his fellow-men.   And thus it came about that, ignoring the very existence of death, since creatures reproduce indefinitely and multiply incessantly, Renoir, like a ship carried to port by winds and the rising tide, attained to a consciousness of eternity.

RENOIR AND TRADITION

MAY be there did not exist in the XIXth century more authentic traditionalists, — men more respectful of forms and institutions, — than the so-called revolutionaries of that period. Revolutionaries despite themselves, those great characters stooped to base and cowardly actions in order to be recognized as orthodox and allowed to pay their respects to the mighty ones of those days. For twenty years Delacroix implored the Institute to grant him a seat; Cézanne's great ambition was to be accepted at « Bouguereau's Salon »; Manet drew away from the company of his friends so as not to alienate official sympathy. Renoir himself was entirely free from worldly ambition, and in fact anything but a careerist. All the same, for twenty years he continued to submit his works to a jury whose own production and principles he despised. Ten times he suffered the insult of being rejected, ten times the injury of having one in three paintings accepted « for a joke » and « hung under the line or skied so high that it could scarcely be seen ». He had a fondness for calling himself « the oldest greybeard among painters » and considered that his being described as a revolutionary was « the most comical thing in the world ».

« I have ever believed, » he said, « and I am still of the same opinion, that I am only continuing what others have done — and much better — before me. » In the preface which he wrote in 1910 to the new edition of Cennino Cennini's *Livre de l'Art,* he wrote : « Though we must guard ourselves against being rooted in the forms we have inherited, we must not, on the other hand, through love of progress, pretend that we can detach ourselves completely from the centuries preceding us. However, this is a manifest tendency with many people, and it is easy to explain the reason why. So many marvellous discoveries have been made during the last hundred years that mankind appears to have forgotten that others lived before. Consequently it is fitting that a man such as Cennini should step forward to remind humanity that it had ancestors who ought not to be treated with disdain. »

By training, Renoir was a traditionalist. At the Ecole des Beaux-Arts, whose teaching he never repudiated, he was an assiduous pupil who « swotted » over studies from the nude and made a serious study of classical art. It was not through a lack of good will that his professor found his painting to be « execrable ». But the most sound quality in Renoir's art had its origin in the museums. As he one day confessed to Vollard, his great discovery was when he came to realize that all that counted for a painter were « the lessons of the art galleries ». Later, he again admits this when saying : « I did not become myself until I once more found my way to the art galleries ». And it was to the Masters of the past that Renoir was continually referring.

« The two most beautiful pictures in the world, » he said, « are the *Embarquement pour Cythère* and Vermeer's *La Dame à la draperie jaune.* » One day, he took the train from Bayreuth (where he had gone to listen to Wagner) for Dresden in order to see *La Liseuse* and also *La Courtisane,* and he regretted his inability to proceed to Vienna, where « there is another Vermeer which has an enormous reputation — *Le Peintre dans son atelier*. I should so much have loved to see that picture!... As in the case of Athens, the whole of my life I have dreamed of going to Vienna. »

Impressionism in its entirety may claim Vermeer as the ancestor of certain of its constituent elements, but Renoir himself can do so more than any other, because he strove not only to solve the problem of representing light, but, in doing so, refused to sacrifice form. Light and form together were the problems which engrossed his mind, and therein we detect the principal difference between his art and that of his friends Monet, Sisley, and Pissarro, who were wholly submissive to reflections, gleams, and irradiations, amidst which form and volume were obliterated. Renoir may also appear, after Vermeer, as the last descendant of Caravaggio. The artistic problem was set for Renoir in the same manner as it was for the followers of that painter, and he responded with the same reflex actions, if not with the same reasoning. The initial act of those who belonged to the School of Caravaggio was revolutionary and destructive : they rebelled against the plastic ideal of the Renaissance, sought to dissolve form in luminous vibrations and the suggestion of movement. That was the « impressionist » part, if one may so express it of Caravaggism. At any rate, such was the general attitude of Impressionism and Renoir until about 1880. Yet Caravaggism also presented a constructive aspect; regarded from that point of view, it came forward with a new conception of form, volume, and relief, which were to be expressed by the sole power of light passing obliquely on to the model, grazing the subject, and issuing from a lateral source. Vermeer rendered whatever rigidity and conventionality might result from this procedure more supple; he introduced atmosphere, connected the objects together, and harmonized them by means of shadings, modulations and other subtle, but essential « passages ». Such was Renoir's own method first when within the impressionist circle, and then, having left it, when he found himself in direct opposition to its destructive character. He continued Vermeer's effort : he was not content with a sliding light, the crude rays of which modelled the form surprisingly; nor was he satisfied to suggest atmosphere merely by coloured waves : he suppressed the very source of light and took it for granted that it resided in the part of the subject which was outside the picture; and thus he was able to bathe his model completely (for we are here considering his portraiture in particular) in a more enveloping light, and with a more diffuse environment. The crisis traversed by Renoir in 1883, when he suddenly went back to Raphael, was, as it were, a resurgence of Romanism, in a Caravaggism unaware of itself, — a verification, a conscience-test, an urge to be convinced of the necessity to maintain reaction, and at the same time a recognition of the frontiers of independence.

The relation between Vermeer and Renoir cannot be said to go as far as manner. The former regarded it as a means of expressing both the volume and the substance of the object : he modelled form from the inside and gradually advanced by tiny, regular strokes of his brush towards the exterior. Whereas Renoir, in whose view touch was primarily dissociation, fusion, and not concentration, ended by dragging together these scattered particles. And eventually, when by dint of hard work he sought more for form and volume, he was quite naturally led to sculpture.

Finally, both of these painters, realizing how transient things are, sought to express the durability of the world, and by their art — the art of Renoir's last years — they succeeded in constructing its magnificent synthesis.

Man of the North as Renoir was, — for that unconscious tendency of his towards the School of Caravaggio only applies to its northern manifestations, — he was tempted not merely by the intimate character of Dutch art, he also came under the seduction of Flemish fecundity. He loved Vermeer's solos, but also the orchestra of Rubens, or, to be more correct, the limited orchestra of Rubens' last years. Renoir had no desire to take part in that struggle between the World and Man which appealed so strongly to the Master of Antwerp, but like the Master of Steen he instinctively directed his steps towards humanity when Man found himself precipitated into the rhythm of the universe and of Nature. Rubens was a man with initiative, vital impulse, and strength in action; Renoir was his replica at the winning-post, and in the place of excesses and exuberance he substituted wisdom and discretion. He listened to the song of Nature, whereas Rubens — authoritative and enthusiastic — roared out his passion for her. Renoir, who remained eternally young, was an ancient Rubens, — that is to say, what Rubens learnt through Life's lessons and in the bitterness of his old age, Renoir possessed as a gift, which he cultivated joyfully. In comparison with the mature Rubens, one may say that Renoir was a contemplative being of the lineage of Vermeer or Titian, whose profound spiritual serenity he was to acquire.

Manifestly and on several occasions, Renoir went for inspiration to Titian and Rubens. We shall shortly have occasion to point out, apropos of the composition of certain portrait-groups, and principally those with two figures, that Renoir often if not invariably squeezed them into a narrow frame, inside which they appeared as half-length portraits. Renoir was, as is well known, an assiduous frequenter of the Louvre; so how can one fail to notice, between *La Loge* and Titian's *La Femme entre deux miroirs,* some curious relationship? Similar intentions are to be detected. In both pictures the man is relegated, anecdotally, to the middle distance, while the beauty and the toilette of the woman, with all her seduction depicted full-face, is set forth in the foreground. Then, there is the same need for the edge of a balustrade at the bottom of the canvas; the same precise visual attention. And the subject itself is analogous, — it has to do with optics and sight : affirmed in the one picture by two mirrors, and in the other by two opera-glasses. The two pictures *Dans la loge,* or *Au concert,* and *L'Allégorie d'Avalos* (both of them more ethereal than the two preceding works) are not without a certain analogy in their composition, — namely, symmetry in the arrangement of the background, profile view of Renoir's little girl with long hair, which is closely allied to the figure of Hymen with unbound locks in Titian's picture; the same need for a round object in the centre, — in the one case a globe and its reflections, in the other flowers; and, finally, the bent arms of the young feminine listener at the concert placed in the centre of the picture after the fashion of the arm of Alphonse d'Avalos. But apart from these details — disconcerting though they are — what is remarkable is the same setting, the same need to fill the canvas and stifle the figures within restricted limits. Renoir often returned to such a presentation, as in *La Conversation, L'Atelier, La Fin du Déjeuner, Au Café, La Première Sortie,* and other pictures, — all of them painted before he became acquainted with Venice.

Nude woman seated (1904).

On going there in 1880, his enthusiasm was boundless. But perhaps he was still more struck by Carpaccio, who, he said, « must have found his models at the fair », and whose naivety delighted him. He saw the works of Titian again in Madrid. « Titian has everything in his favour, » he exclaimed to M. Vollard. « Primarily, mystery... profundity... and then, what nudities!... *Vénus et l'Organiste* — ah! the limpidity of that flesh! One is filled with a desire to caress it ! » Renoir fully identified himself with Titian; the sight of his works and the pleasure he felt when standing before them veritably caused him to live a second life, that of Titian himself when he was giving birth to his masterpieces. He placed him above Velazquez, who, nevertheless, stirred mighty and passionate thoughts in his heart, and taught him supreme dignity, — aristocracy in its minutest detail. Comparing him with Rubens, he said : « Side by side with him, Rubens is outside, and superficial ».

And yet up to what a point has he not placed Rubens under contribution! M. René Huyghe, in a still unpublished lecture devoted to « Rubens and French Art », caught Renoir several times in the very act of borrowing from the Flemish master. The women bearing flowers and fruit in the decorative panel of 1890 are neither more nor less than two of the *Trois Grâces* of Rubens' picture in Vienna; whilst a recollection of the *Jugement de Pâris* of the Prado clearly guided Renoir when he wished to evoke the same scene first of all in his canvas of 1908 and again in his sculpture of 1915-1916, in which he takes from Rubens certain details neglected in the picture. Though the woman on the left differs slightly from his model, the one on the right shows a more striking resemblance, — as, for instance, in the position of the left leg; whilst as regards the legs of the Venus there is again to be found an allied equilibrium; moreover, Renoir introduced into his sculpture the figure of Mercury, which can only have been inspired by the picture in Madrid.

But the somewhat disappointed cry which escaped his lips in the Prado, Renoir did not utter at Munich in 1910, when face to face with *La Tête de Femme,* nor in the Louvre when in front of *Hélène Fourment et ses enfants.* « There is painting for you! » he proclaimed, and what such an exclamation from the mouth of Renoir meant we know full well.

The influence of Rubens made itself felt above all through the intermediary of Watteau. Between *La Kermesse* and *Le Moulin de la Galette* there is the elegance of the XVIIIth century, with its restraint, finish, and deportment. Watteau, Lancret, and Boucher were Renoir's first familiar painters. More directly than from *Le Jardin d'Amour,* Renoir springs from the *Plaisirs du Bal,* disencumbered of flying cupids and heavy decorative detail, — fined down and given a feminine cast. His admiration for *L'Embarquement pour Cythère* was to set the rhythm for several of his pictures, and the seedling may also be detected even in *Le Souvenir de Sorrente.* In *Le Ménage Sisley,* a tender scene in which feminine fears are put to the test of persuasion, — in *La Promenade,* a pressing yet sweet invitation to a young woman who, with her body seen in profile, is turning aside her head, — in *Le Couple dans le Jardin,* a charming amorous attack in the course of which final fears will be swept aside, but thanks to far less brutal weapons than those of the customer in Manet's *Chez le Père Lathuile,* — in all these pictures do we not see modernized details of *L'Embarquement?* What could be more closely related to the feeling of Watteau than *La Partie de Volant,* — the counterpart of the *Divertissements champêtres* of Dresden and elsewhere? The young woman on the left is sister to the dancing-girl in *L'Amour au Théâtre Français* or the *Fêtes vénitiennes,* whilst the group seated on the grass might be listening to some air or other of the XVIIIth century. The fraternity of the two painters is to be detected at every step, despite the phthisis of the one and the health of the other. There is also relationship between the painter of *Le Billet doux* and the one who produced *La Lettre* (of the Paul Guillaume collection), although the latter may have been more expert in cunning and more sensitive to dreamy emotion; whilst blood of the same quality — only more vigorous, more peasant-like in the case of the new style native of Limoges — ran in Renoir's veins as in those of Boucher, whose *La Diane au Bain* was the first picture which « gripped » the future creator of so many *Baigneuses.*

Titian, Rubens, and Watteau, — an admiration for these was mingled with a faithful and unvarying devotion to Delacroix. Renoir copied the latter scrupulously, he sought inspiration from him, tried to discover the secrets of his technique, and until the very end of his days regarded him as his true master. In 1872, Renoir painted after *Les Femmes d'Alger* (« there is no finer picture in the world » he once more exclaimed in his ever renewed enthusiasm), *Les Parisiennes habillées en Algériennes;* and later, about 1875, he copied *La Noce Juive,* after having painted *Une Odalisque.* He paid homage to him again by introducing into the background of portraits, such as that of Mme Chocquet, the sketch of a sconcheon from *Numa et Egérie,* in the Library of the Palais Bourbon, and into another of those of Chocquet himself, who was likewise a whole-hearted admirer of Delacroix, the sketch of a tympanum from *Hercule délivrant Hésione,* in the Salon de la Paix at the Hôtel de Ville. It was Delacroix who threw the door to tradition wide open before Renoir, and, as M. Claude Roger-Marx has written, « what he discovered with so much joy through Delacroix's art (which he adored, whilst holding it at a distance owing to the very rhythm of his own spirit, an enemy to every form of romanticism) was *the craft of Delacroix's masters* », — that is to say, not only Titian and Rubens, but Velazquez and Goya. Signol, his professor at the École des Beaux-Arts, had indeed told him to beware. « Take care you do not become another Delacroix, » he exclaimed on seeing a *poor red* which the young painter dared to put on his canvas. Yet, impenitent, the greybeard of Cagnes was heard one day to say, apropos of a bouquet of dahlias he had just depicted : « Does this not make as brilliant a show as a battle-scene by Delacroix? »

Renoir likewise acknowledged his filiation from the painters of Pompeii, from the Italian masters of the XIVth century, from Raphael, and from Ingres, — at any rate from the Ingres who painted *Mme de Senones* « after the manner of Titian », and *La Source.* But of these masters he was a natural son to a lesser degree, and his uneasy mind directed him to seek for a legal, though temporary paternity which would enable him to contract a fresh union (this time officially sanctioned) with tradition. But in fact, before as well as after this union, Renoir was a member of the great family of genuine artists, — he had merely become acquainted with the other branch of the family, the uncles of the south, and the brothers-in-law of Rome. Nevertheless, his direct descent must be traced from Titian, Rubens, Watteau, and Delacroix, all of whom represented tradition as the heart knows it. And never did Renoir seek to abandon that tradition; on the contrary, he was to still further fortify it by a tradition of the mind. How did he come, indeed, to perfect himself in his art? — By following tradition. Where did he take his favourite promenade? — In the galleries of the Louvre. Where did he find the most reposeful delight? — In the Louvre, « where, on the walls, old friends » were to be found again and again. What did he love most? — « The antique ». Yet many people have understood Renoir only after the manner of that ignorant coxcomb, Comte Isaac de Camondo. « Do you know what Renoir still lacks? » decreed that wealthy collector... « Tradition! One can feel that that man is not a lover of the Louvre! »

RENOIR AND HIS TIME

Pleasure-seeker though Renoir was he lived ascetically. Wholly a man of his period and living intensely, he was the realization of that type of artist who, detached from his period, nevertheless represents and describes it in its very essence. Renoir stood at one and the same time for the political and fashionable, bourgeois and republican *salon* of Mme Charpentier, — for the suburban Sunday of the little employee and a waltz round the room with a little work-girl. Fully aware of the wretchedness of the irregular families of Montmartre, and to such an extent that he was the inventor of those day-nurseries which Mme Charpentier inaugurated later, he remained, however, indifferent to social evolution; and although he was a cuirassier at Bordeaux during the 1870 War, he was unmoved either by the defeat of his country or by the revolution which caused so much blood to flow in Paris. And although, later, in 1910, in his preface to Ceninno Cennini's *Livre de l'Art,* he was to protest against machinism, the division of labour « which has transformed the workman into a mere tool and killed the joy of labour », — although he was to regret the deplorable coupling of man and the machine, and the death of idealism among technicians of the future, Renoir, the painter-monk, was never to be interested in anything save his exclusive passion for art. In truth, it was such painters as Cézanne, Degas, Monet, and Van Gogh, — those who exiled themselves in a sort of private monastery, — who showed the greatest love and comprehension of life.

Ambroise Vollard (1904).
Lithograph.

Renoir's social life was at first that of a needy little employee who, at his office-studio to the very minute and most exact in his work there, went early to bed, after his game of draughts or dominoes. Every form of excess he avoided so as to serve his master the better; but his master was painting, and the narrowness of his existence in those days was gradually enlarged and enlightened. Later, his life became that of a modest middleclass fundholder; and still it was art which engrossed him.

Young Renoir, although born at Limoges on February 25, 1841, was a child of Paris and of the suburbs, a frequenter of the balls on the Boulevards and of the circuses whenever one of these erected its tent at the city-gates. He loved to saunter on the Boulevard du Temple and, fond of melodrama, he was passionately fond, not only of *La Tour de Nesle, Le Bossu,* and *La Dame de*

Montsoreau, but also of Alfred de Musset's comedies, which were then held in great disdain. Young Auguste's ambition was to work at the Sevres Manufactory and become an art-worker, so he entered a studio for painting on porcelain, — a very natural profession for a native of Limoges possessed of taste and certain gifts. Economically and worthily he lived in the Rue d'Argenteuil with his family, the head of which was a tailor in a small way of business. Gounod, at one time, wanted to inveigle his little soloist of Saint-Eustache towards music, and Renoir, who had a sound knowledge of ancient and modern music, retained a desire to be connected with musicians, including Chabrier, Cabaner, and Wagner, whose portrait he painted at Palermo on January 15, 1882, on the day after that on which the great composer completed *Parsifal.*

On becoming a painter, Renoir, ever faithful to the suburbs, removed to Montmartre, and extended his field even to Asnières, where he found both great cordiality and many models. He also aspired to other faubourgs and in particular the faubourg Saint-Germain, where, in the Rue de Grenelle, Mme Charpentier reigned in her *salon.* And there he met the most celebrated men and women of the day in politics, literature and the arts,— Gambetta, Zola, Edmond de Goncourt, Gustave Flaubert, Alphonse Daudet, Huysmans, Théodore de Banville, Carolus Duran, Henner, Jules Ferry, Judith Gautier, Jeanne Samary, Juliette Adam, and Maupassant, whose celebrity filled Goncourt and Zola with jealousy. Not that Renoir had an inordinate love for fashionable gatherings; he merely appreciated them because of the intelligence and the sympathy, as well as the atmosphere of the times to be found there. He often called upon Daudet, whose sensitiveness he so well understood; he was a constant reader of Verlaine; and he came under the influence of the charm of Mallarmé. In his studio of the Rue Saint-Georges there came together a little circle composed of Paul Arène, Norbert Goeneutte, Théodore Duret, Chocquet, Maître Félix Bouchor, Cordey, Lestringuez, Cabaner, and Paul Lhote. At the Café Guerbois, and later at the Nouvelle Athènes, Renoir gladly encountered both the friends of his own studio and those of Mme Charpentier's *salon,* — Mallarmé, Zola, Villiers de l'Isle Adam, Castagnary, Philippe Burty (who wrote critical articles in the *République Française*), Jules de Marthold (who filled the same rôle in the *Monde Thermal*), Jean Richepin (who had just published *La Chanson des Gueux*), Edouard Duranty, Charles Cros (who had just written *Le Coffret de Santal*), and also Manet, Degas, Marcellin Desboutin, Cézanne (but rarely), Guérard (the engraver, who married Eva Gonzalès), — even Gervex and Carolus Duran, who was to fall through ambition. He went there fairly regularly. « He used to arrive, » relates Georges Rivière, who also attended those gatherings, « with hurried step, a serious face, and absent-minded look, because his imagination always carried him far from the place where he might be. Seated in a corner, he rarely took part in the general conversation, and, almost indifferent to what was being said around him, he rolled between his fingers a cigarette, which he frequently allowed to go out; or with the charred end of a spent match he drew some insignificant line or other on the table. » In such a manner it was that Renoir traversed society.

Maupassant, Mallarmé, Verlaine, between these three and Renoir there existed a common comprehension of the times and above all community regarding certain features of the thought of those days. *L'Héritage, Le Baptême, la Femme de Paul, Pierre et Jean* are full of scenes and faces which are, as it were, pictures by Renoir in words. To be sure the Venus of Syracusa, that marble female of which Maupassant makes use, is not Renoir's dazzling woman of flesh and blood, but their method or their lack of theory originated in the same state of mind; both created without disquietude, without coming into conflict with themselves, indifferent as they were to æsthetical and philosophical controversies. Where they differed was in their attitude towards life. As a naturalist incapable of imagination, the author of *Une Vie* accepted reality, was submissive to the world's images as they presented themselves before his registering apparatus, whereas Renoir possessed too great a love not to react in front of Nature, and in the very direction of Nature. He was constantly present in his pictures; he selected what pleased him, was not satisfied with merely looking; he « decoyed the eyes » of the selected model; he poetized, kneaded, or caressed the flesh he was painting. Despite his respect for Nature, he could not prevent himself intervening. Maupassant, on the contrary, was an impassive witness.

Renoir saw Mallarmé chiefly at the house of Berthe Morisot. What he liked in this exquisite artist was « his delightful simplicity ». He willingly acknowledged that « certain poems by Mallarmé were beyond his comprehension, » and he confessed that he preferred Dumas *père*. Yet he « took such a pleasure in seeing him, » for, he added, « though I never understood very much of what he wrote, what a treat it was to hear him speak! » He produced a frontispiece for one of his *Pages,* and the resemblance has already been noted between a nude woman by Renoir and that described in Mallarmé's *Phénomène futur,* — « Some original and naïve folly, an ecstacy in gold, I know not what! in her parlance, her hair, folded with the grace of stuffs around a face lit up by the sanguinary nudity of her lips... And the eyes, comparable to rare stones! which are not worth the look coming from her happy flesh... » The poet of the azure, whom Victor Hugo called his « dear Impressionist poet », and to whom the autumn appeared as though « scattered with freckles », just as *La Promenade* or *La Balançoire* are strewn with touches of gold, was also the author of that poem of Rubens-like procreation and fleshly deception, after the manner of Watteau, — *L'Après-midi d'un Faune.* But Renoir's nymph did not steal away. The Saône, she threw herself into the arms of the Rhône. Venus, chosen by Paris, — she hesitated no more than the shepherd, she advanced without even knowing Rubens' hesitations, — and Bonnard's violence was useless. Renoir was the offering without ceremony, and amiable. But the faun, seeing « an animal whiteness at rest, undulating », « on the blue-grey gold of distant verdure », or admiring « the splendid bath of hair » which disappeared amidst brightness and quivering, « O! ye gems! » seems to describe, under the form of naiades, the women-bathers of Cagnes.

Verlaine's grossness was no more to Renoir's taste than Mallarmé's cerebral perversity. Renoir was neither *fin de siècle,* nor *fin de rac*e. The pantheistic appeals and efforts towards virility of an effeminate period he transcribed into a quiet and healthy plasticity; and thus he held aloof from that decadence whose very name he was ignorant of. He had no need to evoke either the robing-room of Italian comedy, or the masks of the buried past, but was content with a reality as devoid of despair as it was of the idea of forfeiture. To him the flesh had never had the taste of « bitter fruit » which Verlaine experienced; the nobility of Man and his body was intact in the mind of Renoir.

Yet Verlaine and Renoir viewed the human form with similar eyes. They described woman whilst noting the same beloved features, and so long as the poet held himself aloof from vice there was a sensual brotherhood between them. As soon as the oval of a face was sketched in, Renoir placed the light of the eyes; whilst Verlaine strove primarily to be « rich with beautiful eyes », « to believe in large eyes », and to seize « the profound brilliancy of eyes ». Invisibly they were both of them attracted by that liquid brightness, when the picture had been barely begun; and the poet, in his *L'Amoureuse du Diable,* dedicated to Mallarmé, shows her to us :

> « Avec ses cheveux d'or épars comme du feu
> Assise, et ses grand yeux d'azur tristes un peu. »

Moreover, in *Les Fêtes Galantes,* do we not see, even as far as her look is concerned, one of Renoir's models?

> « Blonde en somme. Le nez mignon avec la bouche
> Incarnadine, grasse et divine d'orgueil
> Inconscient. D'ailleurs plus fine que la mouche
> Qui ravive l'éclat un peu niais de l'œil. »

To the desires of these three men, Maupassant, Mallarmé, and Verlaine, — unnatural desires if regarded as being realized to their fullest extent, exaggerated desires because of the very decadence of their spiritual and physical forces, — the desire of one of them for Nature and Reality up to the point when all personality becomes obliterated, in the case of another desire for the liberation of the intellect to the borderland of the impenetrable, and with the third the desire for intimate possession of the created to the extent both of degradation and unstable elevation, — Renoir, the virile man and poet, brought life in the form of power and equilibrium.

Exactly as he had been able to save himself from descending the slippery path of worldliness, so was Renoir able to resist the facility of superficial impressionism. The crisis which, not without difficulty, saved him from this danger was at one and the same time plastic and moral. A parting of the ways, it offered the unsatisfied impressionist the royal road not only of Fragonard and Watteau, but also that of Poussin, the two Le Nain, Rubens and Titian; it pointed out to him the road leading from the pretty to the beautiful, from fluidity to solidity, from the transitory to the eternal, to full-ness, density, grandeur, and the very essence of things. He renounced seduction and skin-deep sensibility for feeling. He rid himself of his femininity. The graph of Renoir's plasticity begins from the plane, passes to atmosphere and then to the limitative line and contour (which enabled him to start on engraving) and finally attains volume and sculpture. Likewise, his moral evolution followed a similar course : he passed from the pleasure of life to the joy of living, from what is necessary and desired to that which is useless, superfluous, superabundant, and gratuitous. But in order to attain what is useless, and indispensable to whomsoever would live humanly, one must consummate the sacrifice, — the Christian sacrifice of renunciation. Nothing is accomplished unless everything, at a certain moment, is brought into question, unless destructive instincts are curbed by discipline, and unless an effort is made.

Renoir did not suddenly awaken to this necessity of reinvigorating his art. It was gradually imposed upon him as he approached the limits of impressionism : objects and methods left him manifestly unsatisfied, and he knew full well that the invariable recourse to incidental effects of light and movement could only lead him to a blind-alley. Renoir did not voluntarily seek as Van Gogh did to attain « great things », but an unconscious need for great things made itself clear to him, — that is to say, a need to draw closer to common-place truth. And deliberately this sensual being, who was thought to have given full rein to facility and to be an enemy to all restraint, placed an iron corset round his body, re-educated his muscles and limbs, rectified his movements, bearing and thoughts.

Some people may have sought to minimize the importance of this crisis and contend that one cannot, on the basis of their treatment, distinguish the canvases before the crisis from works painted afterwards. This remark, which may be upheld to a certain point, indeed reveals in Renoir's case the dissatisfaction of that first stage. Must one go as far as to see a sort of retrograde movement, a renewal, certainly not above impressionism, but through it and within it, during those years when, under the influence of Courbet, rounded masses were already appearing under his planes? Let us merely say that those preliminary trials, corrected and vivified through the liberality of impressio-nism, were resumed at that time on a fresh basis, with a more solid experience and a surer know-ledge both of the strength of the artist and the exigencies of art. And it appears to us to be quite correct to consider the « Nu » of the former Stchoukine Collection dating from about 1875, *La Sortie du Conservatoire* of 1876, or *Les Parapluies* of 1879, as so many normal stages between the *Cabaret de la Mère Anthony* of 1866, the *Après-midi à Wargemont* of 1884, and *La Famille de l'Artiste* of 1896. But one must not forget that *Le Moulin de la Galette* also dates from 1876, and that *La Fin du Déjeuner* and *La Fête de Pan* are also of 1879. Does this mingling of two methods before 1880 prove the fatality of that crisis which acted as a sort of purge, — an elimination of toxines? It was not a question of discontinuance or agreement with traditional æstheticism; but one of exceeding the possibilities of impressionism as regards expression.

M. François Fosca relates, not perhaps without a spice of malice, that it was whilst he was study-ing Delacroix that Renoir discovered Ingres, thus justifying the term invented by Herr Julius Meier-Graefe to designate that crisis, — his « Ingresque period ». Renoir called it his « dry or meagre period ». We ourselves would readily name it his « Mediterranean period » were there not a danger of confusion arising through his Provençal retirement; so we will call it his « Latin period », for to Renoir it was the moment when the nordic and anarchical expression which impressionism is in itself encountered the Mediterranean, Latin spirit of order, and was conquered by it.

Therefore, it was whilst copying *La Noce Juive* in 1875, — that is to say, in the midst of the full impressionist effervescence, — that Renoir may, after some furtive glances, have succumbed to the charm of *Madame Rivière*. With her round face, short nose and bright eyes, the fat and tender Mme Rivière may certainly have seduced the sensual Renoir and drawn him towards Ingres. But the crisis did not begin until 1880.

18

It was in that very year that Renoir painted a portrait of Cézanne. Cézanne and Renoir had known each other since 1863, and Bazille, one day, had been Cézanne's introducer in the studio which the two friends shared. They soon became on very intimate terms; and as soon as Renoir met Chocquet he was instrumental in persuading this collector to purchase one of Cézanne's nudes. Renoir made several sojourns at Aix, in 1886, at the Jas de Bouffan; and on his return from Italy he broke his journey in Provence in order to see his friend. They painted together in the Estaque, on the rocks of which, on one occasion, Cézanne abandoned a watercolour « after having slaved over it for twenty sittings, » — a watercolour which Renoir very piously rescued. For the touchy master of Aix to have given so cordial a welcome to Renoir, a true spiritual sympathy must have existed between them, and there is something symbolic in the sort of visit of homage and gratitude which the Latinized Renoir, on returning to France, paid the Latin master.

It is a fact that the discipline which Renoir imposed on himself was one after the manner of Cézanne, — severe and heroic. He suddenly discovered that he knew « neither how to paint nor draw, » and he then realized that only Latin order could supply him with an easy solution. And that solution Cézanne possessed. More relations existed between Renoir and Cézanne than are generally known. Both had had the same master, Delacroix, and to him they remained faithful from the beginning to the end of their days. They copied him and took his works for the purpose of comparison. Doubtless Renoir demanded from Delacroix the brilliant technique and craft of Rubens and Titian; whereas Cézanne drew from him a spiritual guidance. Yet they were both heirs of the master who painted *Les Femmes d'Alger*. Both of them knew that the lesson of all art was to be learnt in the galleries; and it was in 1883, after having passed near to the painter who gave the often repeated advice « Go to the Louvre» and who said « My desire has been to make impressionism as solid and durable as the art of the galleries, » that Renoir declared, — « I was never myself until I was able to return to the instruction to be found in picture-galleries ». Renoir never, indeed, cast aside that instruction, — what he meant to say was that never until then had he so fully realized its primordial importance. In Cézanne he beheld one who had preceded him amidst the same diffi-

Nude woman in a vineyard (1904).
(Second variant).
Lithograph.

culties when face to face with nature, — one who had been faced with the same problems he himself had tried to solve, — problems of volume, space, composition, and design, — and one who could the most easily enable him to get out of the « blind-alley ».

Renoir was not to follow Cézanne further than that; he was not to experience the whole of the theoretical disquietude of the painter of Aix; he was to solve the problem in another more instructive, simpler, less mental manner. But momentarily their paths ran side by side, at a very essential time for Renoir, and it is necessary to recognise this fact.

At the same time that Renoir's æstheticism was undergoing modification, the character of his life changed. In the same way that the impressionist painter came to understand that a more complete form of art than this existed, so did the suburbanite discover that there were other countries than France. The man whose life had been sedentary suddenly became a traveller. Spiritually as well as physically, Renoir felt a need to move from place to place. Curiosity had taken hold of him. « I have suddenly become a traveller, » he wrote to Mme Charpentier, « and a fever to see the pictures of Raphael has taken possession of me ». We see him travelling backwards and forwards between Paris and Algeria, sojourning in Guernesey, making a lengthy tour in Italy, visiting Spain, Holland, and London. He went in search of advice to countries of ancient yet living art, in the footsteps of Delacroix, — to countries of the art of the Renaissance where Paul Veronese, Titian, Carpaccio and Raphael painted, — to countries where recollections of the art of most ancient times were to be found in the frescoes of Pompeii or in the ruins of Egypt, — and also to countries where the fathers of modern art had flourished, — Rembrandt, Velazquez, Goya, Turner, and Bonington.

But this was not the end of his metamorphosis. The bachelor married (in 1881) and the painter of Montmartre became not only a European but a family artist. At one and the same time his horizon extended and became concentrated, — his affection revived and became fixed. This time, indeed, he entered into a full knowledge of the world and of life.

What did he bring back from Algeria? Very little. He was there in 1879, before going to Italy, and again in 1882, after another Italian visit. However, he found magnificent sun there, the splendour of that Mediterranean atmosphere which clothes ragged beggars in shining mantles, which magically transforms the poor into Emirs, the palms into trees of gold, water into streams of diamonds, and humanity into a kingly community. There he satisfied his delectation as a colourist and could give full reign to his passion for light. But Renoir was seeking for something else — restraint, and knew not how to discover under veiled faces the reflection of the Eternal; nor in the attitude of the Arabs the hall-mark of beauty. All that he could yet see there was a gleam.

Italy alone was a revelation to him, — not merely Venice with which, naturally, he was already in communion, but the Italy of the masters of the XIVth century, of the Farnesian and Pompeïan periods. In the works of the artists of the century of Leo X, he admired, as Georges Rivière tells us, « the serene power, the sober richness of tones, and the linear harmony of great decorative ensembles ». And this intimate friend and biographer adds : « He felt himself at home in that Italy, where, more than anywhere else, in the XVth century, the renaissance of the Greek spirit flourished ». The lesson which Renoir sought in Rome was not merely a technical one, — it was a spiritual lesson; that which he found in the paintings of the Renaissance and in ancient fragments was the proof of divinity. Doubtless the supreme object of an artist's efforts, as he declared to M. Vollard : « must be to strengthen and perfect his craft incessantly ». And it is only, he added, « by tradition that one can succeed therein ». But, he continues, — and the whole passage must be quoted, — « though technique is the basis and the solid part of art, it is not everything. There is something else in the art of the ancients, who made their productions so beautiful; it is that serenity which leads to one never being tired of looking at them, which gives one the impression of something eternal. That serenity was part and parcel of themselves; and it was not merely the result of their simple, quiet life, it was also due to their religious faith. They were conscious of their weakness, so, alike amidst success or defeat, they associated divinity with their acts. God was ever there and Man was of no account. With the Greeks, Apollo or Minerva reigned; whilst the painters of the Giotto period also chose a celestial protector. And thus it was that their works acquired that aspect of sweet serenity which gives them that profound charm and makes them immortal. But man, with his modern pride, is bound to refuse that collaboration, since in his own eyes he is diminished thereby. He has driven God away and in doing so he had driven away happiness... »

After such a profession of faith as this, how is it possible to contend that Renoir was heedless or disdainful of all elevated thought? With Cézanne and Van Gogh he knew full well what our modern world lacks, — a sense of the Divine. To this matter he returns in the preface to Cennino Cennini's *Livre de l'Art,* where he explains that the general value of ancient art resides in « that something which has disappeared — religious feeling, the most fruitful source of their inspiration (i. e., — Cennini's contemporaries). It is that which gives all their works that character of nobility and candour, at one and the same time, and in which we find so much charm... To sum up everything, » he continues, « there then existed between men and the environment in which they moved a harmony born of a common belief... After this one can understand the cause of the general progress in art and of its unity wherever a lofty religious conception holds sway... So much so that one may almost say that, when these fundamental principles are lacking, Art cannot exist ».

Do not these words justify us in saying that the crisis through which Renoir passed was not merely a technical one, but spiritual, philosophical, anti-rationalist, — a crisis of the soul? His desire was « to be touched by grace », so that his mind might receive the god which would animate it. But Renoir did not lose himself on those heights. Raphael's Venus, — she « who comes to supplicate Jupiter », made the same impression upon him as « a good fat gossip on her way back to the kitchen », and he was quite of Stendhal's opinion, that Raphael's women are commonplace and heavy. However, when in Florence, *La Vierge à la Chaise* caused him deep emotion. « I went to see this picture intending to have a good laugh, » he related to M. Vollard. « But behold! I found myself in front of the most free, most solid, most marvellously simple and living piece of painting it is possible to imagine, — a picture with arms and legs of real flesh, and how touching an expression of maternal tenderness! »

Renoir became somewhat rapidly tired with the painting of the Renaissance. « Always the same draperies and the same Virgins! » And he proceeded to Naples for a rest. The art of Pompeii and that of the Egyptians delighted him. He found there Corot's « simplicity of work » and even his silver-grey colour. Face to face with that art he came to understand form and volume; there was no atmosphere, no subtle play of light, no expression of matter; form was wholly created by the relationship between the tones, whilst volume was suggested by modelling and passing touches.

He also took a lesson in pictorial technique which a chance discovery soon developed. For a time it was the technique of fresco-painting which above all occupied his thoughts, and he would no longer work save with red and yellow ochre, green and black terra. On returning to France he painted, after that fashion, at the house of M. Bérard, at Wargemont, two decorations inspired by hunting scenes. Then, one day, in 1883, he chanced to discover in a book-box on the quays a copy of the *Traité de la Peinture de Cennino Cennini, mis en lumière pour la première fois avec des notes par le Chev. J. Tamboni. Traduit par V. M., Paris et Lille, 1858.* The translator was one of Ingres' pupils — Victor Mottez.

Thirty years later, at the request of this painter's son, Renoir consented to write a preface to a new edition of the

Claude Renoir (1904).
Lithograph.

book. When in Rome, Renoir had become greatly interested in the technique of fresco-painting in oils. Now, Cennino Cennini's book revealed to him the methods of the painters of the XVth century, — methods which Mottez had put into practice at Saint-Sulpice, Saint-Germain-l'Auxerrois, and Saint-Séverin. So we see Renoir launched in the direction of pictorial science, and, a passionate beginner in the painting of frescoes, he disdained oils, ignoring, as he himself related later, « the elementary truth that oil-painting must be done with oil ». Like Delacroix and Cézanne, he became anxious as regards the preservation of his materials and sought to prevent their turning black. Doubtless he foresaw that future deficiency in the case of impressionism. The hatred which suddenly took possession of him against impressionism was largely due to its ephemeral character. « The palette of the painters of to-day, » he said, « has remained the same as that of the painters of Pompeii, via Poussin, Corot, and Cézanne, — I mean to say that it has not become enriched... Happy ancients! » he exclaimed on another occasion, — « since they knew the use of only ochres and browns. »

One must try to understand this Jansenist aspiration on the part of a voluptuary as regards colour. Most certainly he did not desire the destruction of the object of his passion; yet he knew it was fraught with danger. There was the temptation of virtuosity. Pompeii and Raphael taught him a lesson in bearing : the inhabitant of the suburbs was on the point of being able to enter the city. But what was that city? Essentially it was the construction of Man made for Man, for the great desire of Man much more than for his satisfaction. For Man's satisfaction is transitory, whereas his invariable desire tends towards the permanence of everything — his desire is one for eternity.

Renoir was seized with that desire for permanency, stability, and the eternal. Now, light appeared to him to be too changeable and fleeting : it differed with every moment and the race was as exhausting as the desperately repeated gesture of the Danaides. To pursue nature in her ever-changing play of light was the height of vanity. Delacroix taught that nature was a dictionary; Corot did not fear to correct it; whilst Cézanne was satisfied to consult it freely. « One must always go back to one's studio, » said Corot to Renoir, who told him the difficulty he felt in working out of doors. Nature will not have her course arrested; in her very essence and in her reflections she is unseizable; she is in a state of perpetual transition. And when man places himself in front of her, he loses his own control. Imprisoned in her light, he comes under the influence of her charm and, sollicited in a thousand manners, finds himself lost in an infinity of sensations. « In the open air, » noted Renoir, « one is captured by light, one has no time to attend to composition. Moreover, out of doors, one cannot see what one does. » One day, to Janniot, he gave the following piece of advice, which in the view of an impressionist is an act of treason, a monstrosity : « A painting is primarily a product of the imagination of the artist and ought never to be a copy ». He confirmed this more precisely when he said : « The atmosphere in pictures is not breathable ».

Did this mean that Renoir was on the point of turning his back on the outside world, shutting himself up in his studio, and disavowing the strength of nature? Writing to Mme Charpentier from Estaque, he said : « I studied deeply in the Naples museums. From every point of view the Pompeian paintings are extremely interesting. I am also remaining in the sun, — not to paint portraits in the full blaze of sunlight; but, whilst warming myself and observing a great deal, to gain, as I believe, the greatness and simplicity of the ancient painters. Raphael did not work out of doors, yet he studied sunlight, for his frescoes are full of it. Thus, through observing the outside world, I have ended by seeing nothing beside the great harmonies, without troubling myself any further over the small details which extinguish the sun instead of setting it in a blaze ».

Thus we see Renoir, at one and the same time led by technical problems and driven on by spiritual needs, reaching towards permanency. And when he had learnt to manufacture that particular atmosphere of pictures, to make it a bond between his imagination and re-created nature, — when he knew how to give life, in that special « environment » of art which is not the « environment » of life, but a transformation, to his figures and nudes, at the same time he discovered the true meaning of art, its conditions, its laws, and its reason. He was then to understand volume and limit, — their necessity and their virtue. He also taught himself composition, which is not merely a coloured and hazardous connection between scattered elements but a well-thought-out piece of construction, — a system which will not permit of the slightest failure; and for nearly twenty years he was to devote himself unwearingly to the painting of his *Baigneuses*, in which he exhausted all the resources of the pyramid, the triangle, and the circle.

Gradually he attained to these pictures of women bathing, among which those of the Tyson Collection mark the summit of his art. After having painted, even in Naples, a nude which is, as it were, purified (1881), he appeared to be unwilling to abandon so rapidly the seductions of impressionism; he only detached himself from it really on account of the human face, the exigencies of which he was obliged to accept. And he again attempted, in rapid succession, the very subject of the *Moulin de la Galette,* but reduced to its principal group, a couple of dancers, — namely, the two paintings called *La Danse à la Campagne* and *La Danse à la Ville* (1883), which constituted three bounds ahead, three jumps from earth towards an ideal. The first of the two *Danse à la Campagne,* in which the male partner is depicted wearing his hat, is the most popular work Renoir ever painted. The village has taken the place of the suburb : the man, a peasant in his Sunday-best, has shed his collar from under a loutish jaw. He is wearing heavy boots and squeezing his partner's arm with a lecherous leer. Where is the elegance of the Don Pedro Vidal de Solares y Cardenas, the seductive gentleman in dung-coloured trousers who dances with Margot at the Moulin de la Galette? He has thrown aside his hat in the other *Danse à la Campagne* and the fan held by his partner is a piece of refinement. We are carried back to the plane of the *Moulin de la Galette,* to comradeship among the sexes, without violence or any ulterior motive. We have passed from a struggle to pleasure, we are coming within reach of respect, tenderness, and homage. We are about to enter the town, but without accepting its hypocrisy. On the contrary, we shall introduce there a frank simplicity and a flavour of cordiality. There we are on the threshold of a world where grace and delicacy reign, — a world of silken dresses and snow-white complexions, amidst that quasi-innocence which envelopes young girls on the occasion of their first fashionable ball.

An innocence which was rather that of ungrateful age than of adolescence; and it was to grow old. The *Après-midi à Wargemont* (1884), which shows the Bérard children on their best behaviour in the parental drawing-room under the supervision of their grown-up sister, bears all the faults of that ingratitude and at the same time allthe hopes of youth. Renoir, in a vacuum, manufactured his own atmosphere and sought for a formula, as Monet, sixteen years before, had sought, by means of an inverse operation, the open-air formula. Impressionism had run its course. And

Lithographic stone with three sketches (1904).

in the portrait of *Lucie Bérard,* it is the whole of modern art in its birth-throes that he calls to his aid — the art of the illuminators, the art of Clouet and Fontainebleau, the art of Piero della Francesca, the art of reflections and transparency, the art of four centuries of effort and glory. The *Baigneuse* painted at Jersey in 1885, was a decorative study, a linear composition, a cartoon for tapestry. That was the period when Renoir was looking towards Versailles, its architectural composition, the ornamentation of its gardens, Girardon's decorative and monumental statuary and the order of a century than which there was none more orderly. For two years he had been haunted by the *Bain de Diane* of the Park of Versailles, which he copied and drew again and again until it became the very source of his inspiration for the *Baigneuses* of the Tyson Collection.

Was Renoir, by attaching himself to classic art and imitating it closely, about to lose his personality? Was he turning into a mere follower, like so many painters? It is only necessary to glance at the *Baigneuses* of the Tyson collection for an answer. Nothing is less servile than this composition, nothing is more modern, — even in the attitudes borrowed from Girardon's low-relief. And notwithstanding his persistent recollection of Diaz's *Baigneuses* (in the Louvre Museum) nothing is more personal. Thus does Renoir prove his own originality, which fears neither the closest comparisons nor the most flagrant plagiarisms. For his own art, that composition was of extreme importance; in that conception, the opposite to that of the *Moulin,* Renoir showed himself to be as

23

sure; he was as free in the open-air as he was in the atmosphere of the picture; he was even more at his ease in the latter, where the air circulates better and is less charged; he succeeded in attaining the same authority whether he was scattering colour or producing with it a synthesis; he was as near the truth whether he was painting a real nature-scene or an imaginary paradise, whether he was representing commonplace gestures or ennobling their movements.

But the Tyson *Baigneuses* have one incomparable advantage : they form an authentic work of art, a creation in all their parts, in all their intentions, in which nothing is left to chance, and in which the painter's most powerful instinct was controlled, not compressed, by his intelligence. There is at first an outburst of abundance (e.g. — the pictures of the former collection of Prince Wagram, 1883), and then they begin to take form, thanks to successive eliminations and siftings. They are the work of a man rich with all his flourishing gifts but also rich through his work, his clear conscience, his will-power, and the full possession of all his faculties, spontaneous or provoked.

That period of respect, which, originating in comradeship, guided Renoir to fraternity, was to brush against a lordly disdainful air. Faces such as those in *La Jeune Fille à la Rose* (1886) and *La Natte* (1887) place a sudden distance between the author and the spectator on the one hand and the model on the other. Woman becomes untouchable and her proud modesty is a rebuff to every desire or indiscretion. Was Renoir, in whose eyes the picture of a nude woman was never complete until he could imagine himself slapping her tighs, to remain long impressed by such superb yet chilling looks?... Those six years of retirement and discipline were sufficient to enable him to acquire that definite certainty, that assurance which enabled him henceforth to overcome all obstacles. He was now able to return to nature; he had travelled through the entire realm of Art; he knew its possibilities in every direction, and would not forget what he had learnt with so much difficulty. Gradually and by easy stages, he connected the severe present with the easy past, without the slightest feeling of remorse or hesitation, but simply with the precautions of a man who knew his way and who put on the brake because he was afraid of outbursts of enthusiasm. But to return was out of the question; it was now a matter of progressing over ground the difficulties of which were known, and without losing the conqueror's rewards. This was the period of such pictures as *Après le Bain* (1888), in which Renoir adapts the seductions of impressionism, in a seductive environment, to strength of drawing, — as *Les Filles de Catulle Mendès* (1888), and the works of 1890 — *Les Jeunes Filles dans les Fleurs, La Baigneuse assise, Les Femmes lisant, La Jeune Fille au Panier de Fleurs,* — paintings of a period of transition and compromise which, through the intermediary of *Jeunes Filles au Piano* (1892) were to lead to those of the fulness of his power.

RENOIR AS FIGURE PAINTER

The last Man died, as it were, with the XVIIIth century; the Individual strove to subsist in Romanticism; and Impressionism appeared to be seized with a desire to give him his quietus, — preceded and aided by Caricature, supported clandestinely by the dissolving action of such pitiless observers as Degas and Toulouse-Lautrec, who set forth man's defects and vices. Man, in Manet's eyes, was but an excuse for showing his wonderful skill as a painter. In the case of Monet and Pissarro and Sisley, he was of the value of a tree-trunk, or a boat on the Seine; he played his little inglorious part as a mere touch of colour in the diffuse whole of a landscape. Nature became void of humanity, — and vegetation took on an air of ennui at being without a master and without a goal. Renoir was the only real impressionist (Degas and Toulouse-Lautrec being of that school only through a spirit of comradeship) who kept in contact with humanity.

More than that : he interested himself in various types of humanity. The humanity of the people and that of the middle-classes. *Le Cabaret de Mère Anthony,* the scenes depicted at La Grenouillère, *Le Moulin de la Galette, Mme Charpentier et ses Enfants,* the behaviour of men in town and country, — all these, from a certain point of view, are human documents; and if these pictures, after some catastrophe, were the only remaining vestiges of society, they would suffice to reconstitute an epoch. They were of that period when Renoir was in the midst of and participating in its social life, and very naturally he came to examine his fellow-citizens very closely.

Throughout his life — and in response to his attitude of the moment — he depicted them under different aspects. He regarded the human being in his relation to nature; he examined him in his relation to his fellow-men : first of all the alliance between man and woman, then man as he is among other men, again when he is with his family, or in a restricted, intimate circle. And he was to end by seeing him merely as a creature in the midst of creation as a whole.

One may say that there is not a work by Renoir which shows indifference towards man. Whereas Pissarro, for example, effaces all trace of man, even to the very fruit of his work, Renoir, on the other hand, always reminds us of his presence : the landscape is a framework for his pleasure and his revels, an accompaniment to the beauty of his form, or an opportunity for him to bury himself amidst nature's charms. The principal personage in Renoir's pictures is never the Seine, or the grass; it is the boating-man standing on the bridge facing the river and the sails, or swiftly sculling on the water; we see the dancer, or the spectator; we see friend talking with friend. During the whole of Renoir's impressionist period we find this feeling of man's domination over nature or woman, but at the same time we note that of love : the woman and the child who make their radiant progress amidst the field of weeds and flowers are in unison with the glory of the humble plants of the meadows.

Rubens and Franz Hals sang the confident and quiet duo of marriage. Renoir renewed it, long before he himself chose a wife. During the whole of his career he hardly ever regarded man as unmarried; and the whole of his work shows constant fidelity to one type of woman, that of his own wife, whoever might be the model he had before him. *Le Ménage Sisley, La Promenade, Les Confidences,* and *Le Couple dans le Jardin,* though their movements sometimes remind us of Watteau, do not display that anxiety and impatience which is shown by the couples in the *Embarquement.* Renoir had no taste for adventure and fugitive experiences; he abbreviated all feminine stratagems; he felt an immediate necessity for confidence. Without a simper, woman must show a happy abandon in the arms of her partner at the dance. *La Loge* transforms Titian's theme — that of coquetry and seduction, pressingly encouraged by man who gained thereby — into an enthusiastic homage towards feminine beauty, adorned without malice or perversion.

Apart from the portrait of man as a social being whom he painted on the spur of the moment at La Grenouillère or in Montmartre, Renoir created a new form of collective portraiture. It was not that of Fantin-Latour when he assembled a number of persons around an idea or a concrete symbol, nor that of Franz Hals and his official assemblies, nor again that of Rembrandt with his groups of business men in consultation. Renoir did not centre a number of sitters around a matter of common interest, or on the occasion of some manifestation, but around friendship. His pretext was a conversation or a luncheon, — with the simple title *La Conversation* or *Le Déjeuner.* Or his subject was *Dans l'Atelier,* which has not the intentional meaning of the Studio at Batignolles; or else *Les Parapluies,* — hardly a pretentious subject; or, once more, *La Sortie du Conservatoire,* an opportunity for bringing young men and maidens together amidst the animation of a competition.

His relinquishment of the modern subject turned him aside from portrait-groups, or at any rate concentrated or restrained that branch of his art. It became portraiture with two sitters, or more if a family link existed between them. Thus we have the portraits of the *Sœurs Lerolle,* reading or playing the piano, of the *Enfants Bérard,* of *Les Filles de Catulle Mendès,* of *Berthe Morisot et sa Fille,* and of *Les Jeunes Filles accrochant des fleurs à leurs chapeaux.* This restriction was a strengthening : these canvases depicting scenes of affection and comradeship became tokens of human feeling. *La Famille Renoir* (1896) was the most tender proof of this.

Family affection — that was the personal and most characteristic sentiment which Renoir reinstalled in art. Impressionism in its entirety was an art of tenderness : the tenderness of Monet and Pissarro towards « fresh woods and pastures new », the stiff yet timid tenderness of Degas towards our poor but arresting humanity, and the suppressed tenderness of Toulouse-Lautrec towards the slaves of pleasure in our large cities. Renoir's tenderness was that of health, — the tenderness of the good companion, the father, brother, or friend, — tenderness towards woman and the mother and, above all, towards children. His work and that of Berthe Morisot together illustrate every phase of family affection.

In his tenderness towards woman, Renoir expressed all his tenderness for the human race; but he saved himself from animality through his predilection (even in the case of his pictures of women bathing) for her face. As he viewed it, the face was the eyes and the mouth, — all the rest was but a caress. The very body of *La Source* or of *Mademoiselle Samary,* the souls of both of them making their appeal through their pupils, is but a support and a spring-board for the eyes. The eyes and the mouth, — that is to say, every woman, however ugly, becomes beautiful and attractive through these. This is the transposition, in the human body, of the whole passion of impressionism : water, light, and reflections. But the eyes and the mouth are the portals of the human being leading towards the soul and into the flesh. Renoir immediately sought for what was most living, most personal, and in the most vulgar of faces he discovered originality. All Renoir's faces are built up for the sake of the eyes and the mouth; the nose is not over important : it is especially devoid of a prominent bony structure, he makes it a discreet connection, an undulating passage between the cheeks; it is a short and even slightly turned up nose so as to leave the lips well disengaged. The foreheads are low so that the hair may accompany at a sufficient distance the brilliancy of the eyes without isolating them or giving them a heavy look. The cheeks are round and commonplace, avoiding all distraction, and the complexion brings forth the full value of lips and pupils.

Woman, as a product of nature, was, in Renoir's eyes, a producer. That was her function. She was a tree which bore fruit. With her strong haunches and ripe breasts, she was ever ready to be fecundated and give birth to little ones. At the sight of woman's tender fruit, Renoir was filled with enthusiasm. A man of nature in his plenitude, he was ready to commune with all the effects of nature. He did not wait to be a father himself in order to love children. His art is not the glorification of the feminine, but a hymn in praise of childhood. What, indeed, he sought to disclose when painting a woman was that which still remained in her from the child she had been — the luminous softness of the skin, her delicate flesh, or, if one may so express it, the character of woman before the fall. Woman who brings forth stands both for what is time-bound and eternal — she is the symbol of the artist's desire to record what is transitory (the sole ambition of impressionism) and to fix what is permanent (the ideal of classicism with its desire for permanence and eternity); she is symbolic of the whole joy of the present, the joy of that reality we can touch and caress, — symbolic, too, of hope in the future, of the pride we take in a continuation of life, of the faun-like desire to procreate, and of the satisfaction there is in survival, — Man's pride when he thinks that thus he has conquered Death.

The child was also an object of meditation to Renoir. First of all and without clearly understanding he looked at other people's children with curiosity, — those, for instance, we see in his pictures of *Mlle Romaine Lanceux* (1864), *La Mère et ses Filles* (1874), in which three pairs of eyes are arranged in a triangle, and *L'Enfant au Polichinelle* (1874), which recalls those lines of Verlaine :

> ... deux bons yeux dans la tête,
> Quelque chose de dur et de doux à la fois.

Then come, like so many pointers towards the future mighty poem in praise of childhood, *Mlle Legrand* (1875), *Mlle Durand-Ruel* (1875), the children of Mme Charpentier (1878), the little girls in the picture *La Pêcheuse de Moules* (1879), *Thérèse Bérard* (1879) and her sisters whom he knew better since he went every year to Wargemont, and where, already, he perceived the astonished yet knowing gravity of children; *La Fillette au Faucon* (1880), *Mlle Grimpel au ruban rouge* and *au ruban bleu* (1880), and *Mlle Irène Cahen d'Anvers* (1880). Baby's first footsteps (depicted in 1878) delighted him in the Luxembourg Gardens (as witness a picture of 1883) he observed the little boys rolling their hoops, and as *La Jeune Mère* of 1881 shows, he already loved to be present at the toilet of the little ones. And then we come to 1885 when he has a child of his own and is about to live in its presence. He was in the very midst of his artistic crisis, — that most serious period of aridity, — when his little Pierre brought him suddenly back to the round, warm reality of his chubby thighs, of his healthy appetite and vitality. Thus the father expressed in painting the eternal poetry of a mother suckling her child in a setting of rural simplicity, and he took such a delight in this new theme of fecundity that he returned to it every year, — and towards the end of his life he was to make it the subject of one of his most magnificent pieces of sculpture. It would seem as though, amidst his formal, almost intellectual preoccupations, the birth of his son recalled to him the existence of the art of Millet, comprehensive of the phenomena of nature and noble human humility.

Renoir closely watched the impetuous and self-willed movements of his child. Once more, he marvelled at the mystery of life when a second child was born to him, and he did not tire at the miracle when Jean was born in 1894. It was a lasting wonder to him. But when Claude was born in 1901 his hymn to childhood burst forth in all its fullness. Renoir did not amuse himself with a child; he did not regard it as a plaything, or a distraction; he took it seriously. He always took everything seriously, and that is doubtless why he loved everything, was never disappointed over anything, and was able to discover joy.

He looked on whilst « Coco » wrote, painted, drew, built houses or castles with bricks or cards, and read. He observed the man in the making, — he followed his metamorphosis. It was a grave matter this growing up of a little boy, in whom the mystery of life — as he learnt what life meant — was developing.

Renoir's artistic progress is punctuated with the feminine figure. Every fresh evolution is illustrated by a nude which appears to play the part of a test or touch-stone on which he tries his art. He made a frank beginning under the protection of Courbet with *La Diane Chasseresse* (1866-67), which was but a nude, as he himself had related, which on grounds of expediency he was obliged to disguise as a mythological goddess, and with *La Baigneuse au Griffon* (1870), which displays its relationship with *Les Demoiselles des Bords de la Seine*. The impressionist period presents nudes only when it reached its zenith : the *Anna* of the Stchoukine Museum (1875), a sister of the surprised Suzannes and crouching nymphs by Rubens, — *La Jeune Fille aux mains dans les cheveux* (Barnes Foundation, 1875), and the Belvédère *Baigneuse* (1876) which Renoir (in that year when he painted the *Moulin de la Galette*) desired to treat solely by means of reflections and a play of light, the two first named pictures remaining still very circumscribed and painted in rounded volumes. It was by a *Baigneuse* painted in Naples that Renoir inaugurated his Latin manner, thereby confessing, perhaps without a thought, the fundamental lacuna in pure impressionism, and finally avowing the relief he felt. At last he could devote himself to the painting of nudes, and without further loss of time he joyously plunged into a deep study of volume, line and composition. It was once more by means of a picture of a woman bathing — *Après le Bain,* of the Oscar Reinhart Collection — that, in 1888, he left that ungrateful period; it is this picture which establishes the new alliance between volume and colour, limit and atmosphere. The painting of the nude was to enable him to attain the fulness of his art, to give him definite stability, to introduce him to the great truths of the Creation, and to place him in possession of the secrets of the fruits of the earth. The *Nu couché* of 1890 shows the serenity of Corot and of his *Bacchante couchée au bord de la mer* (in the Metropolitan Museum, New York); the nudes of 1895, 1902 and 1903 express the repose of certitude; *Les Jeux* and *Baigneuses* of 1897 and 1905 fearlessly add movement to liberated compositions; *La Toilette* (1895-97) again recalls Corot, and has the appearance of being a detail of one of his pictures, — Corot whom he suddenly took to copying, and who, on the eve of his sixtieth year, he was once more to interrogate, as one would a sage of ancient times, as witness his *Ode aux fleurs d'après Anacréon* of 1909 and *Bergers se reposant* of 1911. The *Repos après le Bain* (1909, in the Charpentier Collection) and the *Tasse de Thé* of 1910 evoke Titian and Velazquez with the liberty of one who is their equal. Finally, the closing years, and above all 1916, were to see accomplished what appears to us to be the great natural mystery in the art of Renoir.

THE PAINTER OF THE UNIVERSE

As he approached his sixtieth year, Renoir may be compared to the leader of an orchestra in which all the instruments of the world he had assembled around him are represented by the elements of his art, — colour, design, volume, atmosphere, feeling, and so forth. All the scores of Nature are now familiar to him and henceforth his work is to compose, not mere piano or violin pieces, in colour, drawing, or form, but masterly symphonies which can only be rendered by all those instruments whose sounds, through his gift and long experience, he knows so well how to accord. He is no longer merely a colourist, nor a mere draughtsman; he has become a creator, a conductor of a full orchestra.

Albert André and V. J. Roux-Champion have described how Renoir worked at that period of his life. Drawing, colour and the effects of light grew under his hand simultaneously. First of all he sketched in the outlines of the picture, suggesting the volumes by means of charcoal, sanguine, or a reddish-brown pigment, then with a pure colour thinned with turpentine, he produced a scumble from which emerged a sort of indefinite, iridiscent watercolour on an oil basis. As soon as the turpentine had evaporated, he resumed work with mixture of oil and turpentine and a little more colour; at the same time he added white to the parts which were to be luminous and strengthened the shadows in the same manner.

« Gradually, » continues Albert André, « he made the forms clear, but always allowing them to mingle one with the other. After a few more touches, one saw the beautiful round figures emerge from the coloured fog of the first stage of the picture... » V. J. Roux-Champion adds that the painter's infirmity obliged him « to follow this method more and more, and to such an extent that at the end of his life he hardly used his palette at all for mixing his colours; he did this directly on the canvas. Even after a long sitting his palette remained very clean, — barely spotted with colour; he used it solely for putting pure colours upon it and testing the degree of their fluidity ».

Renoir was never a colourist, either systematically or exclusively. He possessed neither a secret nor a method. To Walter Pach (*Scribner's Magazine, 1912*) who asked him :

« Can you tell me how you produce a red or green tone, for example, so as to obtain your effect? »

« No, » he replied, « I do not know... That has to do with pharmaceutics, — not Art. I arrange my subject as I want it, and then I begin to paint, — just like a child, if you like. Suppose I want a red as clear as a bell. If it doesn't come out like that, I add more red, or it may be another colour, until it is all right. I follow neither rules nor methods. When looking at a nude figure I see myriads of little shades, — and what I have got to do is to select those which, on my canvas, will make that flesh a living, quivering thing. »

He did not know how he did a thing, but the *will-power* to do it was his. He did not begin a picture by making sketches and drawing-in his subject; he set to work to paint there and then; he set this orchestra to play immediately. His palette was then composed of ochres, lac, vermilion, Naples yellow, black and a little white. He impasted only in the case of the high-lights. His technique was that of Delacroix's last pictures.

This final period was not only the natural outcome of preceding years of tireless effort. A new element entered into Renoir's life. Pain and its virtues became known to the pleasure-seeker he had been. As early as 1894, when he was living at the Château des Brouillards, on the Butte Montmartre, he was attacked by a malady which eventually spread to the whole of his body and caused him intolerable suffering. These repeated attacks of articular rheumatism ended in his becoming a complete invalid. He was able to travel less and less, and the day came when he could not even go to Essoye, in the Aube, his wife's native place, where he was so fond of spending month after month. Finally, he buried himself in the South of France, — first of all at Magagnosc, and then, in 1906, at Cagnes. In 1910 he refused to use any more the crutches which had given him the illusion of being able to move about; he renounced every movement save that necessary for the painting of his pictures. From his bath-chair he was carried to his bed and vice-versa. Operations on his foot, knee and hands were performed. His thin and deformed hands were so distorted that the nails would have become embedded in the palms had these not been protected by linen bands. It was in such a state that Georges Besson found him, — with mummified body and a chronic bronchitis which almost choked him, but still working at his pictures. « Between his first finger and thumb, the first joint of which had been disjointed and badly reset, so that it had become spatulate, a brush was stuck after the manner of a pen, » he wrote in the *Revue des Beaux-Arts* of June 16, 1933. « And this brush, after pecking at the palette, worked at great speed on the canvas, and then it was washed in a glass of turpentine to avoid replacing it ».

To physical pain there was soon to be added moral suffering. He lived alone on Les Collettes, at Cagnes, His wife was now dead and his two eldest sons were wounded in the Great War, — « that war », as he said, « which will never end ». He became anxious and nervous and feverish. Yet he continued to paint enthusiastically.

What did the painter with « weakly hands », the bones of which were appearing through the parchment-like skin, paint? Would he attempt to complete his career like Titian, that prince of Venice as well as of painting, a demigod in Olympus? His final triumph was of another kind : it was the triumph that comes with the conquest of suffering. The worshipper of nature fell a victim to nature, and thus he entered all the more closely into communion with her.

Nature, one may well say, had now no more secrets to hold from Renoir. He had instinctively discovered her original principle. Whilst he cannot entirely do without a model to inspire him, that model does not actually have to pose for him. In order to paint a woman or an apple it is sufficient to have before him something already created. Looking at a feminine model he paints fruits, and with fruits before his eyes he paints a nude. All that he needs is the presence of a witness of nature; he requires to be in direct communication with the principle of life. For he knows the common origin of all things and is not embarrassed over their identification. He resumes the revels of his women bathing (1915) and these now become a dance in which the trees, the water and the air — elements of harmony — participate. All these rhythms of form and colour the painter arranges in accordance with life; without an effort he comes back to the antique attitude; and attains to the inner meaning of things.

All the realms of creation are under his power. He is no longer a painter but an artist; he no longer knows what it is to be a colourist. He can speak as powerfully with a simple line, or mere form. Painting, engraving, sculpture, — everything is the same to the creator : it is all alluvium and everything will be grown there. Incapable of using his hands, he can sculpture exactly as the leader of an orchestra plays. V. J. Roux-Champion has described him, armed with a stick, in the act of directing his assistants, first of all Guino and then Maurel, — stimulating or moderating their work as sculptors. « Remove those muscles! — make those things more rounded! Add more clay. More! Still more! But there you must take it away. Beware of dryness, — think of the outer covering! » And so we see him — he who always, like Van Gogh, regretted the disappearance of studios and collective work, who denounced this as the cause of the decadence of art, and who thought a resurrection was impossible — brought through his infirmity to attempt a collaboration between the creator and the executant. That simple trial, those half dozen statues marked the birth of a whole current in modern sculpture, — that of Maillol, Joseph Bernard, Gimond, their pupils and their successors.

Renoir went still further than this. The greater he was the more humble he became. To be the leader of an orchestra is to be outside the ranks. Yet he wished to remain in the ranks. No more was it his desire to mould nature according to his will; his sole wish was to be a creature among creatures; he identified himself with the fruits of the earth; his poor body became thinner and thinner, less and less subject to his desires, almost completely independent of himself; he became, as it were, an old and knotted and twisted vine-plant, or some almost century-old tree. Death in his case was a coalescing with the fraternity of nature. When dead, Renoir was verily a creator, — one inseparable from the rest of creation and who, at last, was to realize his love of art in its entirety.

BIBLIOGRAPHY

BOOKS

Philippe BURTY : Préface à la vente du 24 mars 1875, à l'Hôtel Drouot.

DURANTY : La nouvelle peinture, Paris, E. Dentu, 1876.

Théodore DURET : Les peintres impressionnistes, Paris, H. Heymann and J. Pérois, 1878.

Théodore DURET : Critiques d'avant-garde, Edit. Charpentier, 1885, pp. 109-116 (reprint of the foreword to the catalogue of the Renoir exhibition, Durand-Ruel, 1883).

Félix FÉNÉON : Les Impressionnistes en 1886. Publications de la Vogue, 1886.

Georges LECOMTE : L'Art impressionniste, Paris, Chamerot et Renouard, 1892, in 4°.

Arsène ALEXANDRE : Préface à l'Exposition particulière de Renoir, chez Durand-Ruel, 1892.

Gustave GEFFROY : Histoire de l'Impressionnisme. La Vie artistique, third series, 1894.

André MÉLLERIO : L'Exposition de 1900 et l'Impressionnisme, Floury, 1900, in-8°.

Camille MAUCLAIR : L'Impressionnisme, Librairie de l'Art ancien et moderne, 1904, in-8°.

Camille MAUCLAIR : Les Maîtres de l'Impressionnisme, leur histoire, leur esthétique, leur œuvre, reprinted by Ollendorf, Paris, undated.

Julius MEIER-GRAEFE : Entwicklung und Geschichte der modernen Kunst, Stuttgart, Jul. Hoffmann, 1904.

Théodore DURET : Histoire des peintres impressionnistes, Floury, 1906.

Wynford DEWHURST : Impressionist painting, London, G. Newnes, 1904.

Exhibition of Impressionists at the Grafton Galleries, London, 1905.

Octave MIRBEAU : Renoir, Edit. Bernheim Jeune, 1913. Foreword by Pascal Forthuny and texts by 58 writers, extracted from articles or books. (A. Wolff, Philippe Burty, Castagnary, Téodor de Wyzewa, G.-Albert Aurier, Benjamin Constant, Cézanne, Bourdelle, etc.).

Albert ANDRÉ : Renoir. Edit. Cahiers d'Aujourd'hui, Crès, 1919, 1923-1928, in-4°.

Ambroise VOLLARD : La vie et l'œuvre de Pierre-Auguste Renoir, Paris, Vollard, 1919, in-4°.

Maurice DENIS : Théories, 4th edit., Rouart and Watelin, 1920.

Ambroise VOLLARD : Renoir, Crès, 1920.

Renoir Exhibition at Oslo, Stockholm, Copenhahagen, 1920.

G. RIVIERE : Renoir et ses amis, H. Floury, Paris, 1921, in-4°.

François FOSCA : Renoir. Coll. Maîtres de l'Art moderne, Rieder, 1923.

RENOIR, Peintre du Nu, published by Bernheim Jeune, 1923.

Georges DUTHUIT : Renoir. Les Contemporains, Stock, 1923, in-18.

Loys DELTEIL : Le Peintre-Graveur, Vol. XVII (Pissarro, Sisley, Renoir), published by the author, 1923.

Théodore DURET : Renoir. Bernheim Jeune, publ. 1924, in-4°.

Gustave COQUIOT : Renoir. Albin Michel, 1925, in-12.

Adolphe BASLER : Pierre-Auguste Renoir. Les Peintres français nouveaux, Gallimard, 1928, in-12.

Léo STEIN : A. Renoir. Les Albums d'Art, Druet, 1928, in-4°.

Paul JAMOT : La Peinture française au Musée du Louvre, Ecole française, Part Three, published by L'Illustration, Paris, undated.

Julius MEIER-GRAEFE : Renoir. Klinkhardt und Biermann, Leipzig, 1929, in-4°.

Jean ALAZARD : L'Orient et la Peinture française au XIXe siècle, d'Eugène Delacroix à Auguste Renoir, Plon, 1930, in-4°.

Albert ANDRÉ : L'Atelier de Renoir, publ. by Bernheim Jeune, Vol. I, 1931, infolio.

Marc ELDER : L'Atelier de Renoir, publ. by Bernheim Jeune, Vol. II, 1931, in-folio.

Elie FAURE : Renoir. Recueil de fac-similés de dessins. Publ. by Crès.

Jacques-Émile BLANCHE : Les Arts plastiques (La IIIe République, de 1870 à nos jours), preface by Maurice Denis, 1931, in-8°.

Robert REY : La Peinture française à la fin du XIXe siècle. Renaissance du sentiment classique. Publ. by Van Oest, 1932 (chapter on Renoir, pp. 43 to 59).

Georges BESSON : Renoir. Les Artistes nouveaux, publ. by Crès, 1932, in-12°.

Georges BESSON : L'Impressionnisme et quelques précurseurs (Lettres de Renoir), Braun, 1932.

Albert ANDRÉ and Georges BESSON : Catalogue of the Renoir Exhibition (with letters), Galeries Braun, 1932-33.

Claude ROGER-MARX : Renoir. Coll. Anciens et Modernes, publ. by Floury, 1933, in-8°.

Charles STERLING : Catalogue of the Renoir Exhibition, Musée de l'Orangerie, Edit. des Musées Nationaux, 1933, Preface by P. Jamot.

Elie FAURE : Préface du catalogue de l'Exposition d'œuvres des dix dernières années (1909-1919) de Renoir, Paul Rosenberg, 1934.

Paul JAMOT : La Peinture en France, pp. 207 to 215, Plon, 1934.

Raymond COGNIAT : Préface et Catalogue de l'Exposition Renoir, l'œuvre sculpté, l'œuvre gravé, aquarelles et dessins, « Beaux-Arts », Paris, undated.

The Renoir Exhibition, Gall. Read and Lefevre, London, 1935.

Charles BERNARD : Catalogue de l'Exposition des Impressionnistes, Brussels, 1935.

A. VOLLARD : Souvenirs d'un Marchand de tableaux, Albin Michel, 1937, *passim*.

ARTICLES

Arsène HOUSSAYE : L'Artiste, novembre 1877.

L'IMPRESSIONNISTE, Journal d'Art : Edit. by Georges Rivière. Five issues published in the spring of 1877.

Edmond RENOIR : Lettre adressée à Emile Bergerat. Vie moderne, No 11, 19th June, 1879, p. 174

Théodore de WYZEWA : L'Art dans les deux Mondes, 26th December, 1890.

André MELLERIO : L'Art dans les deux Mondes, 31st January, 1891.

Emil WALDMANN : Die internationale Kunstausstellung in Bremen. Kunst und Künstler, April, 1910, pp. 370-373.

Louis VAUXCELLES : L'Art à Paris. Drawings by Renoir. L'Art moderne, 14th July, 1912, p. 219.

J.-E. BLANCHE : Sur les routes de la Provence, de Cézanne à Renoir. Revue de Paris, 15th January, 1915.

Arsène ALEXANDRE : Renoir sans phrases. Les Arts, No 183, 1919, pp. 2-10.

Georges LECOMTE : L'Œuvre de Renoir. L'Art et les Artistes, 1920, No 4, pp. 143-150.

Gustave GEFFROY : Renoir, peintre de la femme. L'Art et les Artistes, 1920, No 4, pp. 151-162.

Paul JAMOT : The Acquisitions of the Louvre during the War, Burlington Magazine, November, 1920, pp. 219-220.

Pierre du COLOMBIER : Renoir. Revue critique, 25 th January, 1920. pp. 152-162.

J.-E. BLANCHE : La technique de Renoir. L'Amour de l'Art, February, 1921, pp. 38-40.

Joachim GASQUET : Le paradis de Renoir. L'Amour de l'Art, February, 1921, pp. 41-45.

A. VOLLARD : Renoir et l'Impressionnisme. L'Amour de l'Art, February, 1921, pp. 46-53.

Paul VALERY : Souvenirs de Renoir. L'Amour de l'Art, February, 1921, p. 54.

Waldemar GEORGE : Cézanne et Renoir. L'Amour de l'Art, February, 1921, pp. 55-58.

F. FOSCA : Les dessins de Renoir. Art et Décoration, October, 1921, pp. 97-108.

Jens THIIS : Renoir. Atlantis (Norway), No 3, 1921, pp. 115-137.

Paul JAMOT : Renoir. Gazette des Beaux-Arts, November-December, 1923, pp. 257, 281 and pp. 321-344.

P. DUMAS : Quinze tableaux inédits de Renoir. Renaissance de l'Art français, July, 1924, pp. 361-368.

Léon WORTH : La Collection Gangnat. L'Amour de l'Art, February, 1925, pp. 41-56.

Raymond BOUYER : Les Renoir de la Collection Gangnat. Gazette des Beaux-Arts, April, 1925, pp. 246-250.

TERNOWIETZ : Le Musée d'Art Moderne de Moscou. L'Amour de l'Art, December, 1925.

Georges BESSON : Renoir à Cagnes. Beaux-Arts, June, 1933.

F. FOSCA, Ph. D. and R. C. : Triomphe de Renoir. Beaux-Arts, June, 1933.

René HUYGHE : Conclusion à l'Exposition Renoir. L'Amour de l'Art, October 1933.

Kenneth CLARK : Burlington Magazine, 1935.

Jules JOËTS : Les Impressionnistes et Chocquet. Lettres. L'Amour de l'Art, 1935.

Maurice BÉRARD : La Famille Bérard, private edition, 1937.

Michel FLORISOONE : Renoir et la Famille Charpentier. Lettres inédites. L'Amour de l'Art, February, 1938, pp. 34-40.

THE WORKS

PORTRAIT OF SISLEY
Photo Hyperion

SELF-PORTRAIT OF THE ARTIST
Photo Durand-Ruel

PORTRAIT OF Mʀ. CHOCQUET
Photo Durand-Ruel

PORTRAIT OF CLAUDE MONET
Photo Durand-Ruel

PORTRAIT OF EDMOND RENOIR, THE ARTIST'S NEPHEW
Photo Durand-Ruel

PORTRAIT OF CLAUDE MONET
Photo Arch. Phot. d'Art. et d'Histoire

PORTRAIT OF Mʀ. FOURNAISE

Phot. Arch. Phot. d'Art et d'Histoire

PORTRAIT OF CAPTAIN DARRAS
Photo Durand-Ruel

PORTRAIT OF A VEILED YOUNG LADY
Photo Hyperion

PORTRAIT OF FREDERIC BAZILLE
Photo Arch. Phot. d'Art et d'Histoire

PORTRAIT OF RICHARD WAGNER
Photo Arch. Phot. d'Art et d'Histoire

PORTRAIT OF A WOMAN
Photo Druet

PORTRAIT OF MADAME GEORGES CHARPENTIER
Photo Druet

PORTRAIT OF MADEMOISELLE B.
Photo Durand-Ruel

PORTRAIT OF MADEMOISELLE M. D. R.
Photo Durand-Ruel

WOMAN WITH A RED BODICE
Photo Durand-Ruel

HALF-LENGTH PORTRAIT OF JEANNE SAMARY
Photo Hypérion

ON THE SEA-SHORE
Photo Hypérion

YOUNG GIRL CARRYING A BASKET OF FLOWERS
Photo Durand-Ruel

HEAD OF A WOMAN
Photo Durand-Ruel

YOUNG GIRL WITH A HAT
Photo Durand-Ruel

PORTRAIT OF MADAME J. DURAND-RUEL
Photo Durand-Ruel

PORTRAIT OF JEANNE
Photo Jos. Hessel

YOUNG GIRL SEATED
Photo Druet

PORTRAIT OF THERESE BERARD
Photo Hypérion

HALF-LENGTH PORTRAIT OF A WOMAN
Photo Durand-Ruel

PORTRAIT OF BERTHE MORISOT AND HER DAUGHTER
Photo Durand-Ruel

PORTRAIT OF JEAN RENOIR
Photo Durand-Ruel

PORTRAIT OF JEAN RENOIR HOLDING A HOOP
Photo Durand-Ruel

A CHILD DRAWING
Photo Durand-Ruel

COCO WRITING
Photo Durand-Ruel

PORTRAIT OF JACQUES FRAY
Photo Druet

PORTRAIT OF " COCO "
Photo Hyperion

65

PRAYER
Photo Durand-Ruel

PORTRAIT OF CLAUDE RENOIR
Photo Durand-Ruel

HEAD OF A LITTLE BOY
Photo Durand-Ruel

PORTRAIT OF JEAN RENOIR SEWING
Photo Durand-Ruel

A YOUNG BOY
Photo Durand-Ruel

A WASHERWOMAN AND HER CHILD
Photo Durand-Ruel

THE ARTIST'S FAMILY
Photo Durand-Ruel

PORTRAIT OF LUCIE BÉRARD
Photo Hyperion

YOUNG GIRLS AT A PIANO
Photo Druet ·

YOUNG GIRLS LOOKING AT AN ALBUM
Photo Durand-Ruel

THE GUITAR PLAYER
Photo Durand-Ruel

WOMAN PLAYING THE GUITAR
Photo Durand-Ruel

WOMAN SEATED AMONGST FLOWERS
Photo Druet

WOMAN IN THE GARDEN
Photo Druet

THE END OF THE LUNCHEON
Photo Druet

WOMAN WITH A FAN
Photo Hyperion

THE JEWISH WEDDING (after E. Delacroix)
Photo Durand-Ruel

YOUNG GIRLS PLAYING AT BATTLEDORE AND SHUTTLECOCK
Photo Durand-Ruel

THE CHILDRENS' AFTERNOON AT WARGEMONT
Photo Nitzche

84

THE CHARPENTIER FAMILY
Photo Durand-Ruel

A BOX AT A CONCERT
Photo Durand-Ruel

THE BOX
Photo Durand-Ruel

ROWERS AT LUNCHEON
Photo Durand-Ruel

AT THE " MOULIN DE LA GALETTE ,,
Photo Hyperion

LEAVING THE CONSERVATORY
Photo Durand-Ruel

UMBRELLAS
Photo Durand-Ruel

AT THE CAFÉ
Photo Druet

HER DÉBUT
Photo Durand-Ruel

PORTRAIT OF MADAME MAITRE
Photo Durand-Ruel

THE SISLEY HOUSEHOLD
Photo Arch. Phot. d'Art et d'Histoire

DANCING IN THE COUNTRY
Photo Durand-Ruel

DANCING IN THE TOWN
Photo Durand-Ruel

THE MUSSEL GATHERER
Photo Druet

THE SERVANT
Photo Durand-Ruel

SPRING-TIME

Photo Druet

WOMAN GATHERING FLOWERS
Photo Druet

THE WHITE DOG
Photo Druet

TWO YOUNG WOMEN IN THE GRASS (a detail)
Photo Druet

YOUNG GIRL SEATED
Photo Durand-Ruel

THE COIFFURE
Photo Hyperion

WOMAN WITH A STRAW HAT
Photo Durand-Ruel

YOUNG GIRL WITH A STRAW HAT
Photo Durand-Ruel

ROWERS AT CHATOU
Photo Durand-Ruel

CLAUDE MONET PAINTING IN HIS GARDEN
Photo Durand-Ruel

THE PLACE DE LA TRINITE IN PARIS
Photo Durand-Ruel

THE PONT NEUF IN PARIS
Photo Durand-Ruel

LANDSCAPE AT ANTIBES
Photo Durand-Ruel

THE CHURCH AT CAGNES
Photo Hyperion

WOMAN IN RED IN A LANDSCAPE
Photo Jos. Hessel

THE FARMERHOUSE AT CAGNES
Photo Durand-Ruel

THE SEINE AT ARGENTEUIL
Photo Durand-Ruel

THE GRENOUILLERE
Photo Durand-Ruel

" LES COLLETTES „ AT CAGNES

THE COUNTRY-HOUSE
Photo Durand-Ruel

THE SEINE AT CHATOU
Photo Durand-Ruel

LANDSCAPE
Photo Hyperion

A VIEW OF NAPLES
Photo Durand-Ruel

VENICE
Photo Durand-Ruel

A STEEP ROAD AMIDST TALL GRASS
Photo Arch. Phot. d'Art et d'Histoire

A MOSQUE AT ALGIERS
Photo Durand-Ruel

A WOMAN READING
Photo Durand-Ruel

THE SHEPHERD
Photo Durand-Ruel

BATHER
Photo Druet

THE « GRANDE BAIGNEUSE » WITH CROSSED LEGS
Photo Hyperion

GETTING-UP
Photo Durand-Ruel

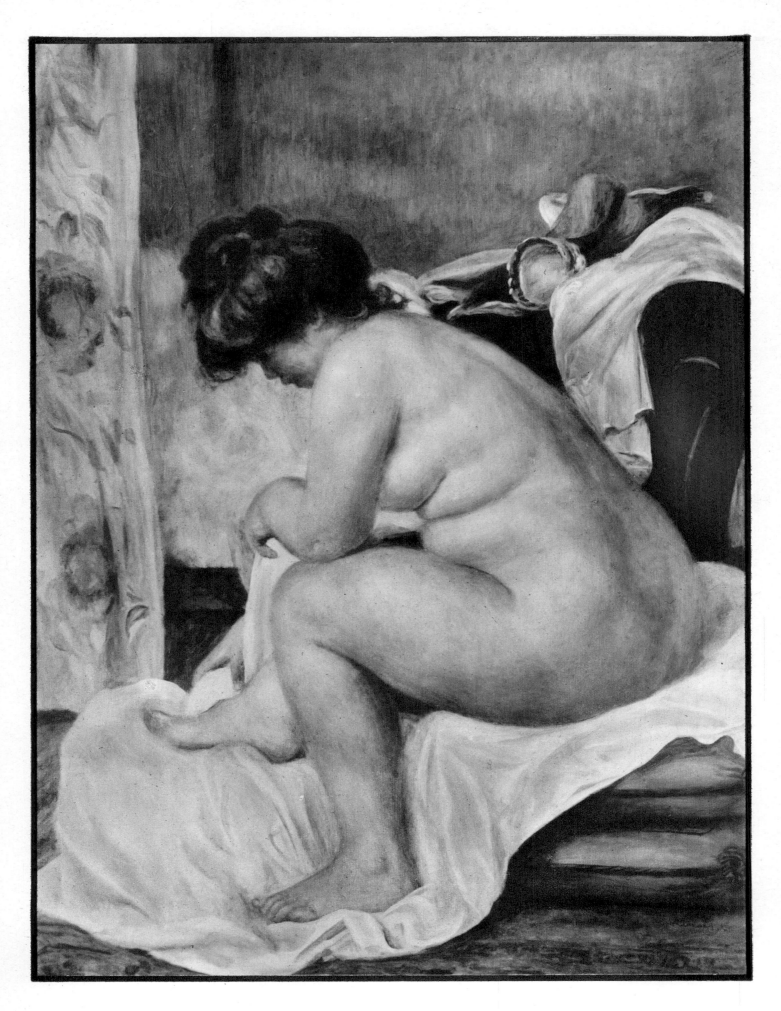

AFTER THE BATH
Photo Durand-Ruel

BATHER
Photo Bulloz

BATHER DRYING HERSELF
Photo Durand-Ruel

A BATHER STANDING
Photo Durand-Ruel

BATHER
Photo Durand-Ruel

AFTER THE BATH
Photo Durand-Ruel

THE TOILET

Photo Hyperion

THE TOILET : A WOMAN COMBING HER HAIR
Photo Durand-Ruel

WOMAN DRESSING HER HAIR
Photo Durand-Ruel

NUDE WOMAN RECLINING
Photo Durand-Ruel

BATHER
Photo Durand-Ruel

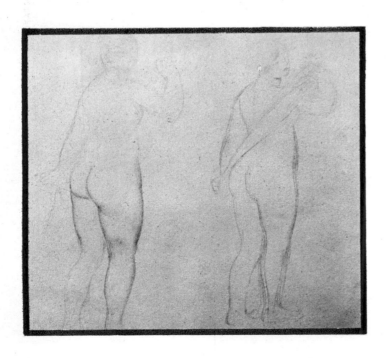

A BATHER SLEEPING
Photo Durand-Ruel

RECLINING WOMAN
Photo Durand-Ruel

THREE-QUARTER VIEW OF A BATHER
Photo Durand-Ruel

GABRIELLE WITH A ROSE
Photo Hyperion

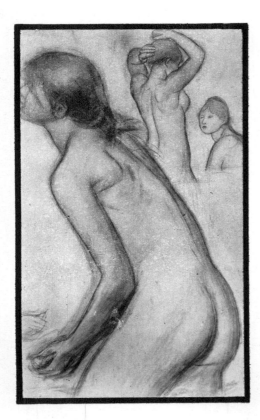

STUDIES FOR " LES GRANDES BAIGNEUSES „
Photo Durand-Ruel

STUDIES FOR " LES GRANDES BAIGNEUSES ,,
Photo Druet

LILAC
Photo Durand-Ruel

GLADIOLI
Photo Durand-Ruel

ROSES IN A VASE
Photo Durand-Ruel

ANEMONES
Photo Rosenberg

A VASE OF FLOWERS
Photo Durand-Ruel

CHRYSANTHEMUMS
Photo Hyperion

JAPANESE MEDLARS
Photo Durand-Ruel

STRAWBERRIES AND SUGAR-BASIN
Photo Bernheim Jeune

155

MELON AND FRUIT
Photo Durand-Ruel

PHEASANT, FIELD DUCK AND THRUSHES
Photo Durand-Ruel

SUGAR-BASIN, GLASS AND LEMON
Photo Durand-Ruel

A LEMON AND A COFFEE-POT
Photo Durand-Ruel

VENUS TRIUMPHANT
Photo Hyperion

RENOIR AND HIS CRITICS

Before passing in review the attitude assumed by those who have criticised Renoir's work, would it not serve a useful purpose if we dwelt for a while on the subject of Renoir himself as a critic? Renoir, indeed, wrote a few critical articles in that journal *L'Impressionniste* (copies of which are now exceedingly rare) which was under the editorship of his friend Georges Rivière. This ephemeral publication — it lived only twenty-one days — undertook to defend the new school against the sarcastic remarks of the public and the insults of the Institute. Renoir published in it first of all a short letter addressed to his « dear friend » Rivière,— a letter modestly signed « Un peintre ». His subject was architecture in general and the new Louvre in particular, — that new Louvre which, although copied from the old one, he found was ugly, « because its ornamentation is heavy, commonplace, and the work of artisans chosen haphazard, whereas that of the old Louvre is light and was carried out by true artists. The ornamentation of the Ministry of War is still more deplorable than that of the new Louvre : the building is overloaded with monstrosities... The groups arranged on the façades of the Opera or perched above it do not appear to form part of the building; they are more of an encumbrance than an ornamentation.

« All this is worthy of being carefully studied in detail; I should like to guide your readers before all these buildings erected so profusely in our streets under the Second Empire; I should like to make them understand — an easy thing to do — what a difference there is between the buildings of past centuries and those of our days. »

It was in the third issue of the little review that Renoir furnished a proof of his fidelity towards tradition. And the first page of this number, by the by, was devoted to a pen-and-ink sketch of his picture *The Swing*.

Encouraged by Rivière, Renoir continued his contributions in the fourth number of *L'Impressionniste,* and this time it was indeed painting — « Contemporary Decorative Art » — which interested him. His fairly long article was written with so deep a knowledge of his subject that it is necessary to quote a few passages.

Renoir began by pointing out that « the paintings in the Opera do not harmonize with the building. Those of Baudry — pale and weak, lacking in colour and strength — disappear amidst the gilding and the lights. Pils' ceiling stands out better, but he has derived a spurious strength from his recollections of Delacroix, translated, as it were, by a sick man. In short, his work forms an extensive stain, wearisome and even vulgar, in the midst of the luxury with which it is surrounded. The other paintings of the Academy of Music all display analogous defects. Their authors fixed their thoughts on the work of the Venetian or German painters, on that of Delacroix and Ingres. Not one of them knew how to be a decorative artist.

Their works are easel-pictures on a grand scale, painted in accordance with academic principles... Delacroix alone, in our times, understood the art of decoration... consequently his paintings at St. Sulpice are masterpieces... The value of decorative painting lies in the fact that it is polychromatic; the more varied and harmonious the tones are in a painting the more decorative it will be. For instance, mosaic does not need to depict a subject, as long as the arrangement of its colours is harmonious it possesses a value. The stained-glass windows of the Middle-Ages are beautiful because they are in harmony with the buildings for which they were made and because they possess incomparable richness of colour. »

These wise words of an artist who was destined to become a superb decorator are followed by a keen onslaught against the instruction given to architects, painters and sculptors at the École des Beaux-Arts, — instruction « entirely based on the past ». — « Finally, » adds Renoir, « I should like to say in conclusion that, until a new generation of architects has arisen to replace the present coterie by a new education, the control of a building under construction ought to be placed in the hands of painters ».

No useful purpose would be served by reproducing in these pages all the insults and stupidities which have appeared — and still continue to appear — on the subject of Renoir's art. Not indeed that interesting studies and sound pieces of criticism are lacking. We have merely made a selection, and are of the opinion that the simple publication of these various commentaries will suffice to make it clear under what conditions — often heroic and always painful — the impressionists in general and Renoir in particular had to work.

After the first exhibition, in 1874, of the « Société anonyme des Artistes-Peintres, Sculpteurs et Graveurs », which was the occasion for much jesting, after the fashion of Louis Leroy's humorous article in *Charivari,* the second exhibition of 1876 provoked a storm of furious protests.

« Instead of softening the angles, » wrote Charles Bigot in those days, « and occupying themselves with the acquisition of the qualities they lack, these painters appear to work merely with the object of displaying their defects, to aim more and more at scandal. It is excusable to fire a single pistol shot to attract the world's attention, but at the tenth shot only idlers pay attention, and at the twentieth even these have disappeared. »

Albert Wolff discoursed on nothing less than madness :

« These so-called artists call themselves members of the uncompromising set, or impressionists. Seizing hold of canvases, colours and brushes, they daub a few tones haphazard and sign their names underneath! In a similar manner, at Ville-Evrard, lunatics pick up pebbles from the roadway and imagine that they have found diamonds. A terrible spectacle of human vanity straying to the borderland of madness... But try to explain to M. Renoir that the torso of a woman is not a mass of flesh in a state of decomposition, with green and violet patches which denote a complete state of cadaveric putrifaction... you might as well waste your time in explaining to one of Dr. Blanche's patients, who thinks he is the Pope, that he really lives in Batignolles and not at the Vatican. »

Edmond Duranty, in a pamphlet entitled *La Nouvelle Peinture : à propos d'un groupe d'artistes qui expose dans les Galeries Durand-Ruel* (published by Dentu), attempted to defend his friends, but so tepidly that really he succeeded only in instilling doubt in the minds of some who were sympathetic towards the new school, — an attitude, it is said, which this critic borrowed from Degas.

« Originality is mingled with eccentricity and ingenuousness, » he wrote; « visionaries are found side by side with profound observers, — naive blockheads side by side with savants who would re-discover the artlessness of the ignoramus There are truly delightful pieces of painting for those who can recognise them side by side with unfortunate experiments which set one's nerves on edge. »

Duranty concludes with this maritime metaphor : « A few of the boats are very small and narrow and suitable only for coastal navigation. But let us think, on the contrary, in the case of the art of painting, of a long sea voyage ».

In the spring of 1877 there was a fresh exhibition, this time called « Exposition des Impressionnistes », organised by G. Rivière of *L'Impressionniste, journal d'art,* on Renoir's suggestion. This was also the year when Ludovic Halévy produced at the Théâtre des Variétés his play *La Cigale,* in which he brings on to the stage an impressionist painter, at whom he pokes gentle fun.

At this exhibition in the Rue Le Peletier, Renoir exhibited his *Bal du Moulin de la Galette* and *La Balançoire.* Following the example of Albert Wolff and *Le Figaro,* the whole of the Parisian press attacked Renoir and his friends. On this subject, here is what the *Impressionniste* wrote in its first and second issues :

« Apart from *Le Rappel, L'Homme Libre* and a few other journals, the entire press is unanimous in its recriminations. In *Le Figaro,* amongst other papers, the criticism is unworthy of the clever man who signed the article. »

« On April 8, *Le Pays* published a stupid article grouping all the impressionists together, distorting the names, attributing the works of one painter to another, speaking ill of all of them for no understandable reason, confounding men of the most varied talent, — in brief, displaying how lightly the article had been written, without the slightest regard for justice and truth... *La Petite République Française* dared to print a somewhat anodyne criticism, and would willingly have spoken well of the exhibition if influential critics had not done their best to damn it. »

The following is a specimen of what *Le Pays* published on April 9th :

« It appertains to madness; it is a deliberate excursion into the realm of the horrible and the execrable. One might surmise that all these pictures had been painted with closed eyes by the insane, who on tin palettes mixed, haphazard, the most violent colours. It is the very opposite of what is permissible in painting, the contrary of what is called light, clearness, transparency, shade and drawing. At first one smiles, but on leaving it is with a feeling of intense sadness. One's impressions are identical with those after a visit to Sainte-Anne or to Ville-Evrard. »

Barbouillotte, in the *Sportsman* for April 7th, perpetrated the following execrable joke :

« It is impossible to stand for more than ten minutes before some of the most sensational of the pictures in this gallery without immediately evoking a recollection of sea-sickness. Involuntarily we think of a certain luncheon we had before going on board on a beautiful spring morning, — a luncheon composed of strawberries and cream which was not able to support the pitching of the vessel; and that is perhaps the reason why some art-lovers were heard to remark : ' One cannot deny that there are some things here which have been brought up very well ' ».

Roger Ballu, in *La Chronique des Arts et de la Curiosité,* passed judgment on Renoir in the following manner :

« In *La Balançoire* and *Le Bal du Moulin de la Galette* the same M. Renoir set himself the task of copying nature servilely. One's first impression is that some accident must have happened to his pictures on their way from his studio to the exhibition. For they are spotted with round marks, with here and there what look like stripes. However, on examining them carefully we begin to see what their author wanted to do, — he tried to render the effect of full sunlight pouring through foliage on to people sitting under the tree. The round marks are supposed to be the shadows cast by each leaf, — a truly impressionist feat, I must confess. But on undertaking such a struggle with nature, do we not expose ourselves to an inexcusable and senseless defeat, for the very good reason that such an undertaking will never be anything save ridiculous? »

In the *Impressionniste* of April 6th, Georges Rivière took up the defence of his friend Renoir, generously and sincerely, but in a somewhat featureless manner :

« Certainly M. Renoir has a right to be proud of his *Bal :* he was never better inspired; his picture is a page of history, a precious token of Parisian life, and rigorously exact in every detail. Nobody before him ever thought of recording on a canvas of such large dimensions one of the events in our daily life, — a piece of boldness which will meet with a well-deserved success. This picture will have a very important bearing on the future and we make a point of stressing this. It is an historical work. »

Philippe Burty (in *La République Française* of May 27th, 1879) wrote :

« M. Renoir, after too many long years of waiting, attains success. In our opinion he tarried too long over making necessary concessions to firmness of touch. His portrait of our friend Spuller, formerly exhibited with the « Intransigeants » was not born from so sober a palette as this huge and harmonious portrait of Mme Georges Charpentier and her children. »

From the pen of Castagnary, writing in *Le Siècle,* on the occasion of the 1879 Salon, came the following :

« In the foremost rank of those who trouble themselves over the new spirit and seek in everyday events subjects for a wholly original, non-imitative art, one must place M. Renoir. No one has fewer visible connections than he has. From what source does he spring? There is no school can claim him as its own, and he is as equally free from tradition... Sometimes we have seen him in the company of the impressionists, and this contributed to a certain misunderstanding as regards his manner; but he did not tarry among them unduly, and it is now at the Salon, together with the majority of artists, that he has just demanded his share of publicity. The critics cannot fail to be favourable towards him. »

In *Le Temps* of April 19th, 1880, Paul Mantz wrote :

« In the presence of the works of certain members of the group, one is inclined to suspect some physical defect of the eye, — some peculiarities of vision which, whilst providing oculists with a joyful subject for study, would be the cause of consternation in family life. »

In Joris Karl Huysmans' *L'Art Moderne,* apropos of the Exposition des Indépendants of 1882, we read the following estimate of Renoir's work, — Renoir « a gallant and adventurous charmer » :

« In 1877 I once more came across Renoir with more solidly constructed works, — their colouring more definite and distinguished for a more sure feeling for modernity. Certainly — and despite the fact that visitors laughed like a flock of cackling geese in front of these pictures — his paintings revealed a precious talent. Since then M. Renoir appears to me to have established his position definitely... His *Femme à l'éventail* of the present year — with that fine sparkle in her large black eyes — is delightful. I am less taken, for instance, with his *Déjeuner à Bougival*. A few of his boating-men are good; but none of the women is charming. The picture is not strong enough. These girls are dainty and full of gaiety, but they do not exhale the perfume of the daughters of Paris; rather are they springtime wenches who have just landed from London. »

Téodore de Wyzewa, in 1891, wrote :

« One can recognise M. Renoir's soul in its entirety in his flower-pieces, — the most beautiful pictures of flowers which have ever been painted, so marvellously alive are they, so full of colour, and always so attractive through a wholly feminine mingling of sweet languor and unsettling caprice. »

From Arsène Alexandre's preface to the catalogue of the Renoir exhibition at Durand-Ruel's this passage may be selected :

« As to his drawing, which Renoir's most bitter adversaries have never dared, even in heroic days, to question, it possesses the grace we associate with childhood. Truly do we find there those treasures of a gifted child. His drawing is that of a master-painter who, amidst the bitterness of life and anxieties of an artistic career, was able to preserve entire the candour and vivacity of impression of the twentieth century. »

In 1892, G. Albert Aurier wrote :

« Possessed of such ideas, and with such a vision of the world and femininity, it was to be feared that Renoir would create merely a *pretty,* merely a *superficial* art. But he was never superficial. On the contrary, he is profound, for, though this artist has almost entirely suppressed intellectuality in his sitters, he has, by way of compensation, been lavish with his own intellectuality. As to *prettiness,* this is undeniably to be found in his work; but how different *this* prettiness is to the insupportable prettiness which is practised by fashionable painters. »

The Caillebotte Bequest was the occasion, on March 9th, 1897, for the following outburst in the *Eclair* :

« The State protects such rubbish as this! The Luxembourg Gallery is a school. What instruction our young artists will henceforth receive there! A pretty state of things this! All of them will now begin to paint impressionist pictures! Ah! these people think that they are painting Nature, — Nature which is so admirable in all her manifestations. What pretention on their part! Nature is not for them. Take M. Monet, for example, — you will remember his cathedrals. Just think that formerly he knew how to paint. Yes, I have seen good things from his brush, but now... And is there not also a M. Renoir, — yes, *noir* (black) he is well called; and he never knew how to hold a pencil! He is not like the other, Renouard, — *nouard*. »

An extract from an article in *Le Temps* of March 9th, 1897 :

« ... That veritable malefactor who has turned artistic youth crazy, without the excuse of sincerity as in Manet's case, or of Monet's unreflecting enthusiasm. »

Then, in *La Revue du Palais* of October 1st, 1898, come these lines by Benjamin Constant :

« It is odious to hear this incessant chatter about the impressionist school, as though impressionism could represent a school of painting. What? — the art which gave us Clouet, Poussin, Lesueur, Claude Lorrain, Lebrun, Largillière, Rigaud, Watteau, David, Prud'hon, Gros, Géricault, Ingres, Delacroix, Baudry, and Meissonnier is out of date? It is true that not one of these painters looked at Nature through a prism; they left that new fashion of expressing light to the decadents of our day... Consequently impressionism appears to us, in brief, to be a school of snobs, the laiety, the conscious or unconscious enemies of art; and its days appear to be numbered. »

Charles Morice's opinion (*Mercure de France*, December 1st, 1905) was summed up as follows :

« His nude women are gardens... the sensuality which these fleshly gardens awakens is merely gluttony. I believe that there are two forms of art, just as there are two of love; and that particular way of loving — delicious though it may be — is not great art. »

Cézanne, through the intermediary of Emile Bernard (*Mercure de France,* October, 1907), said :

« ... Pissarro drew near to nature; Renoir created the woman of Paris; Monet supplied vision. What follows does not count. »

According to Albert Besnard (1913) « Renoir was the only French painter who, through his genius knew how to replace drawing by colour. »

Pierre Bonnard (1913) declared « ... I profess admiration and veneration for his genius. »

Bourdelle's tribute in 1913 was « Nobody is more human, modern and sensitive in his art than the painter Renoir, and thus nobody resembles the ancient decorators more than he. »

Thadée Natanson (1913) said :

« It was the longest and the happiest reign — even near to that of Rubens or that of Hokusai — one can instance among the masters of painting. »

In the catalogue for the Exhibition of French Art, at Christiania, in 1919, Henri Matisse wrote :

« His work displays to us an artist who was possessed of the greatest gifts and who gratefully respected them. »

Miguel Zamacoïs, in *Candide,* of June 22nd, 1933, declared :

« It is understood that one must be an incorrigible ignoramus not to be able to appreciate a fine Renoir of the ' best period ' at its true value.... Unfortunately there was his second manner, — that of intensive production, — the lamentable period of hard labour during which the old and faltering painter scrubbed and scrubbed on his canvases, and turned out a whole series of repetitions in which we can distinguish Renoir with a mixture of Julienne soup, or Russian salad, or red-current jam. And these are openly recognised by disinterested and impartial art-lovers, if not by the dealers in this costly merchandise. »

Writing in *Le Figaro,* in August, 1933, Mme Gérard d'Houville said :

« What are his subjects and models? Doubtless that was of little moment to him... Hence, bad taste and an innocent vulgarity which strikes, if not connoisseurs, at any rate the profane — among whom I am to be counted. He possesses nothing of that distinction which palliates Manet's most striking or out-of-date examples of ugliness. »

And this is how Mme Gérard d'Houville — a worthy successor of Albert Wolff — describes one of Renoir's pictures :

« A group of Pomonas — inflated pneumatic figures, smeared with a sort of reddish oil — are reclining in an orchard, where they appear to be ripening, and are wholly resigned to their fate of becoming monsters prior to being eaten. »

Clearly we have not yet come to the end of the misrepresentation of Renoir's work. But, in conclusion, let a most intelligent and just judgment — that which M. Paul Jamot pronounced in the catalogue of the Renoir Exhibition of 1933 — be quoted :

« Less classical in formation and even in taste than Degas, but perhaps more traditionally instinctive, Renoir finds his way back again to eternal classicism by another path... Though through a lingering prejudice he continued to give the title of *Baigneuses* to his beautiful feminine nudes reclining on the sea-shore or on the sward of Elysian fields, these are indeed nymphs and goddesses whose amiable and glorious company he incessantly increased. They are more and more foreign to those pictures of modern woman in a state of nudity which are the only ones permissible in realism; they can lay claim to a much finer patronage — that of Corot, Titian, and Giorgione. »

DETAILED DESCRIPTION
OF THE PLATES AND REPRODUCTIONS

33. PORTRAIT OF SISLEY, 1868. Canvas, 0.80 m. by 0.65 m. Ch. Pomaret, Paris. Photo Hypérion.

34. SELF-PORTRAIT OF THE ARTIST, 1897. 0.41 m. by 0.33 m. Durand-Ruel, New York. Photo Durand-Ruel.

35. PORTRAIT OF MR. CHOCQUET, 1876. Canvas, 0.46 m. by 0.36 m. Oskar Reinhart, Winterthur. Photo Durand-Ruel.

36. PORTRAIT OF CLAUDE MONET, 1872. Canvas, 0.60 m. by 0.48 m. Arthur Sachs, New York. Photo Durand-Ruel.

37. PORTRAIT OF EDMOND RENOIR, THE ARTIST'S NEPHEW, 1908. Canvas, 0.55 m. by 0.46 m. Formerly Ed. Renoir's coll. Photo Durand-Ruel

38. PORTRAIT OF CLAUDE MONET, 1875. Canvas, 0.83 m. by 0.60 m. Musée du Louvre, Paris. Photo Arch. Phot. d'Art et d'Histoire.

39. PORTRAIT OF M. FOURNAISE, 1880-1881. Canvas, 0.55 m. by 0.46 m. Formerly M. Fournaise's coll. Photo Durand-Ruel.

40. PORTRAIT OF CAPTAIN DARRAS, 1871. Canvas, 0.81 m. by 0.65 m. Staatliche Gemäldegalerie, Dresden. Photo Durand-Ruel.

41. PORTRAIT OF A VEILED YOUNG LADY. Canvas, 0.61 m. by 0.51 m. Musée du Louvre, Paris. Photo Hypérion.

42. PORTRAIT OF FREDERIC BAZILLE, 1868. Canvas, 1.065 m. by 0.74 m. Musée du Louvre, Paris. Photo Arch Phot. d'Art et d'Histoire.

43. PORTRAIT OF RICHARD WAGNER, 1893. Replica. Canvas, 0.41 m. by 0.32 m. Musée de l'Opéra. Photo Arch. Phot. d'Art et d'Histoire.

44. PORTRAIT OF A WOMAN, 1875. Canvas. Barnes Foundation, M rion, Pa., U.S.A. Photo Druet.

45. PORTRAIT OF MADAME GEORGES CHARPENTIER, circa 1877. Canvas, 0.48 m. by 0.40 m. Musée du Louvre. Photo Druet.

46. PORTRAIT OF MADEMOISELLE B., 1898. 0.41 m. by 0.32 m. Durand-Ruel, Paris. Photo Durand-Ruel.

47. PORTRAIT OF MADEMOISELLE D. R., 1882. Canvas, 0.65 m. by 0.54 m. Private collection, U.S.A. Photo Durand-Ruel.

48. WOMAN WITH A RED BODICE, circa 1916. Canvas, 0.41 m. by 0.33 m. Photo Durand-Ruel.

49. HALF-LENGTH PORTRAIT OF JEANNE SAMARY, 1877. Canvas, 0.56 m. by 0.46 m. Musée d'Art Occidental, Moscow. Photo Hypérion.

50. ON THE SEA-SHORE, 1883. Canvas, 0.92 m. by 0.73 m. Metropolitan Museum of Art, New York. Photo Durand-Ruel.

51. YOUNG GIRL CARRYING A BASKET OF FLOWERS, circa 1890. Canvas, 0.81 m. by 0.65 m. Private collection, U.S.A. Photo Durand-Ruel.

52. HEAD OF A WOMAN. Canvas, 0.41 m. by 0.32 m. Photo Durand-Ruel.

53. YOUNG GIRL WITH A HAT. Canvas. Photo Durand-Ruel.

54. PORTRAIT OF MADAME J. DURAND-RUEL, 1911. Canvas, 0.92 by 0.73 m. Private collection, U.S.A. Photo Durand-Ruel.

55. PORTRAIT OF JEANNE. Canvas, 0.46 m. by 0.38 m. Félix Gouled, New York. Photo Jos. Hessel.

56. YOUNG GIRL SEATED, 1909. Canvas, 0.655 m. by 0.545 m. Musée du Louvre, Paris. Photo Druet.

57. PORTRAIT OF THÉRÈSE BÉRARD. Canvas, 0.55 m. by 0.47 m. Mme Thurneyssen. Photo Hypérion.

58. HALF-LENGTH PORTRAIT OF A WOMAN, 1917. Canvas. Private collection. Photo Durand-Ruel.

59. PORTRAIT OF BERTHE MORISOT AND HER DAUGHTER, 1894. Canvas, 0.81 m. by 0.65 m. Ernest Rouart, Paris. Photo Durand-Ruel.

60. PORTRAIT OF JEAN RENOIR, circa 1906-1907. 0.41 m. by 0.325 m. Private collection. Photo Durand-Ruel.

61. PORTRAIT OF JEAN RENOIR HOLDING A HOOP, 1899, Canvas, 0.66 m. by 0.50 m. Durand-Ruel, New York. Photo Durand-Ruel.

62. A CHILD DRAWING, 1888. Canvas, 0.26 m. by 0.43 m. Durand-Ruel's private collection. Photo Durand-Ruel.
    HEAD OF A CHILD. 0.32 m. by 0.29 m. Private collection. Photo Durand-Ruel.

63. « COCO » WRITING, 1910. Canvas, 0.365 m. by 0.48 m. Private coll. Photo Durand-Ruel.
    A CHILD ASLEEP. Private collection. Photo Druet.

64. PORTRAIT OF JACQUES FRAY, circa 1912. Canvas, 0.42 m. by 0.33 m. Mme Val, Paris. Photo Druet.

65. PORTRAIT OF « COCO », 1896-1899. Canvas, 0.41 m. by 0.32 m. L. A. Gaboriaud, Prais. Photo Hypérion.

66. PRAYER, circa 1890. Canvas, 0.41 m. by 0.32 m. Private collection. Photo Durand-Ruel.

67. PORTRAIT OF CLAUDE RENOIR. Canvas, 0.30 m. by 0.27 m. Private collection. Photo Durand-Ruel.

68. HEAD OF A LITTLE BOY, 1895. Canvas, 0.22 m. by 0.16 m. Private collection, New York. Photo Durand-Ruel.

69. PORTRAIT OF JEAN RENOIR SEWING, circa 1904. Canvas, 0.55 m. by 0.46 m. Private collection. Photo Durand-Ruel.

70. A YOUNG BOY, 1890. Canvas, 0.41 m. by 0.32 m. Private collection. Photo Durand-Ruel.

71. A WASHERWOMAN AND HER CHILD, circa 1886. Canvas, 0.81 m. by 0.65 m. Private collection. Photo Durand-Ruel.

72. THE ARTIST'S FAMILY, 1896. Canvas, 1.70 m. by 1.35 m. Barnes Foundation, Merion, Pa., U.S.A. Photo Durand-Ruel.

73. PORTRAIT OF LUCIE BÉRARD, 1884. Canvas, 0.35 m. by 0.27 m. Maurice Bérard, Paris. Photo Hypérion.

74. YOUNG GIRLS AT THE PIANO, 1892. Canvas, 1.16 m. by 0.88 m. Musée du Louvre, Paris. Photo Druet.

75. YOUNG GIRLS LOOKING AT AN ALBUM, 1899. Canvas, 0.31 m. by 0.65 m. Private collection U.S.A. Photo Durand-Ruel.

76. THE GUITAR PLAYER, 1897. Canvas. 0.81 m. by 0.65 m. Durand-Ruel's private collection, Paris. Photo Durand-Ruel.

77. WOMAN PLAYING THE GUITAR, 1897. Canvas, 0.81 m. by 0.65 m. Private collection. Photo Durand-Ruel.

78. WOMAN SEATED AMIDST FLOWERS, 1882. Canvas. Formerly Bernheim Jeune collection. Photo Druet.

79. WOMAN IN THE GARDEN, 1873. Private collection. Photo Druet.

80. THE END OF THE LUNCHEON, 1879. Canvas, 0.99 m. by 0.82 m. Staedelsches Kunstinstitut, Francfort-on-the-Mein. Photo Druet.

81. WOMAN WITH A FAN, 1881. Canvas, 0.65 m. by 0.54 m. J. Laroche, Paris. Photo Hypérion.

82. THE JEWISH WEDDING (after Delacroix), 1870. Canvas, 1.09 m. by 1.45 m. Formerly Jean Dolfus' collection. Photo Durand-Ruel.

83. YOUNG GIRLS PLAYING AT BATTLEDORE AND SHUTTLE-COCK, 1886. Canvas, 0.54 m. by 0.65 m. Durand-Ruel, New York. Photo Durand-Ruel.

84. AFTERNOON AT WARGEMONT, 1884. Canvas, 1.27 m. by 1.73 m. National Gallery, Berlin. Photo Nietzsche.
    A BASKET OF FLOWERS, 1890. Canvas, 0.65 m. by 0.81 m. Private collection. Photo Durand-Ruel.

85. THE CHARPENTIER FAMILY, 1878. Canvas, 1.545 m. by 1.90 m. Metropolitan Museum of Art, New York. Photo Durand- Ruel.
    HALF-LENGTH PORTRAIT OF A YOUNG GIRL. Pastel, 0.30 m. by 0.24 m. Private collection. Photo Durand-Ruel.

86. A BOX AT A CONCERT, 1880. Canvas, 1.00 m. by 0.80 m. Private collection, U.S.A. Photo Durand-Ruel.

87. « LA LOGE », 1874. Canvas, 0.80 m. by 0.64 m. Samuel Courtauld, London. Photo Durand-Ruel.

88. ROWERS AT LUNCHEON, 1881. Canvas, 1.28 m. by 1.73 m. Philips Memorial Gallery, Washington. Photo Durand-Ruel.
    ROWERS. Pastel, 0.46 m. by 0.59 m. Private collection. Photo Durand-Ruel.

89. AT THE « MOULIN DE LA GALETTE », 1877. Canvas, 0.78 m. by 1.14 m. Musée du Louvre, Paris. Photo Hypérion.

90. LEAVING THE CONSERVATORY, 1876. Canvas, 1.95 m. by 1.15 m. Formerly P. Cassirer collect., Berlin. Photo Durand-Ruel.

91. UMBRELLAS, 1879. Canvas, 1.80 m. by 1.15 m. National Gallery, Millbank (Tate Gallery), London. Photo Durand-Ruel.

92. AT THE CAFÉ, 1876-1877. Private collection. Photo Druet.

93. AT THE CAFÉ, 1876. Canvas, 0.65 m. by 0.50 m. National Gallery, Millbank (Tate Gallery), London. Photo Durand-Ruel.

94. PORTRAIT OF MADAME MAITRE, 1871. Canvas, 1.30 m. by 0.83 m. Formerly Pellerin collection, Paris. Photo Durand-Ruel.

95. THE SISLEY HOUSEHOLD, 1868. Canvas, 1.05 m. by 0.75 m. Walraf-Richartz Museum, Cologne. Photo Arch. Phot. d'Art et d'Histoire.

96. DANCING IN THE COUNTRY, 1883. Canvas, 1.80 m. by 0.90 m. Durand-Ruel, Paris. Photo Durand-Ruel.

97. DANCING IN THE TOWN, 1883. Canvas, 1.80 m. by 0.90 m. Durand-Ruel, Paris. Photo Durand-Ruel.

98. THE MUSSEL-GATHERER, 1895-1898. Replica. 0.56 m. by 0.46 m. Formerly Laroche collection, Paris. Photo Druet.

99. WOMAN SWEEPING, 1898. Canvas, 0.65 m. by 0.46 m. Private collection. Photo Durand-Ruel.

100. SPRING-TIME, circa 1878. Canvas, 0.60 m. by 0.50 m. Formerly Bernheim Jeune collection, Paris. Photo Druet.

101. WOMAN GATHERING FLOWERS, 1872. Canvas, 0.65 m. by 0.54 m. Private collection, U.S.A. Photo Druet.

102. THE WHITE DOG. Canvas, 0.28 m. by 0.41 m. Mme Hüe, Paris. Photo Druet.
HEAD OF A CHILD. 0.30 m. by 0.25 m. Private collection. Photo Durand-Ruel.

103. TWO YOUNG WOMEN IN THE FIELDS. A detail. 1875. Canvas, 0.74 m. by 0.60 m. Barnes Foundation, Merion, Pa., U.S.A. Photo Druet.
VEILED WOMAN. Pastel, 0.56 m. by 0.48 m. Formerly Ring collection, Berlin. Photo Durand-Ruel.

104. YOUNG GIRL SEATED, circa 1880. Canvas, 0.62 m. by 0.50 m. Private collection, U.S.A. Phot Durand-Ruel.

105. THE COIFFURE, 1888. Canvas, 0.81 m. by 0.58 m. Durand-Ruel, Paris. Photo Hypérion.

106. WOMAN WITH A STRAW HAT, 1901. Canvas, 0.50 m. by 0.61 m. Formerly Oscar Schmitz collection. Photo Durand-Ruel.
HEAD OF A YOUNG GIRL. Black pencil drawing, 0.58 m. by 0.43 m. Durand-Ruel, Paris. Photo Durand-Ruel.

107. YOUNG GIRL WITH A STRAW HAT, 1878. Pastel, 0.46 m. by 0.61 m. Private collection, U.S.A. Photo Durand-Ruel.
HALF-LENGTH PORTRAIT OF A YOUNG WOMAN. Canvas, 0.55 m. by 0.46 m. Private collection. Photo Durand-Ruel.

108. ROWERS AT CHATOU, 1872. Canvas, 0.81 m. by 1.00 m. Adolphe Lewisohn, New York. Photo Durand-Ruel.

109. CLAUDE MONET PAINTING IN HIS GARDEN, circa 1878. Canvas, 0.50 m. by 0.61 m. Private collection, U.S.A. Photo Durand-Ruel.

110. THE PLACE DE LA TRINITÉ IN PARIS, 1882. Canvas, 0.54 m. by 0.65 m. Formerly Hazard collection. Photo Durand-Ruel.

111. THE PONT-NEUF IN PARIS, 1872. Canvas, 0.74 m. by 0.93 m. Formerly Ralph. M. Coe's collection, Cleveland, Ohio, U.S.A. Photo Durand-Ruel. *Marshall Field Collection*

112. LANDSCAPE AT ANTIBES, 1900. Canvas, 0.65 m. by 0.81 m. Mrs. Chester Beatty, London. Photo Durand-Ruel.
LANDSCAPE. 0.24 m. by 0.46 m. Photo Durand-Ruel.

113. THE CHURCH AT CAGNES, 1905. Canvas, 0.41 m. by 0.33 m. Durand-Ruel, Paris. Photo Hypérion.

114. WOMAN IN RED IN A LANDSCAPE. Canvas, 0.46 m. by 0.55 m. Félix Gouled, New York. Photo Jos. Hessel.

115. THE FARM-HOUSE AT CAGNES, 1915. Canvas. Private collection. Photo Durand-Ruel.

116. THE SEINE AT ARGENTEUIL, 1878. Canvas, 0.54 m. by 0.65 m. Private collection. Photo Durand-Ruel.
WHITE HOUSE IN A LANDSCAPE, 1895. Canvas, 0.20 m. by 0.31 m. Private collection. Photo Durand-Ruel.

117. THE GRENOUILLÈRE, 1868. Canvas, 0.65 m. by 0.92 m. Oscar Reinhart, Winterthur. Photo Durand-Ruel.
THE GRENOUILLÈRE, 1873. Canvas, 0.46 m. by 0.55 m. Formerly Thomson collection, Hambourg. Photo Durand-Ruel.

118. « LES COLLETTES » AT CAGNES, 1908. Canvas, 0.40 m. by 0.53 m. Formerly Gangnat collection. Photo Durand-Ruel.
HOUSE AT GAGNES. Canvas, 0.14 m. by 0.20 m. Private collection. Photo Durand-Ruel.

119. THE COUNTRY-HOUSE, 1914. Canvas, 0.54 m. by 0.65 m. Private collection. Photo Durand-Ruel.
NEIGHBOURHOOD OF BRIEY. 0.32 m. by 0.41 m. Private collection. Photo Durand-Ruel.

120. THE SEINE AT CHATOU. Canvas, 0.73 m. by 0.92 m. Private collection. Photo Durand-Ruel.
LANDSCAPE AFTER COROT, 1898. Canvas, 0.40 m. by 0.55 m. Private collection. Photo Durand-Ruel.

121. LANDSCAPE. Canvas, 0.30 m. by 0.30 m. Renand collection, Paris. Photo Hypérion.

122. A VIEW OF NAPLES, 1881. Canvas, 0.58 m. by 0.80 m. Formerly E. Bérard, Paris. Photo Durand-Ruel.

123. VENICE, 1881. Canvas, 0.54 m. by 0.65 m. Formerly Hirschmann's collection. Photo Durand-Ruel.

124. A STEEP ROAD AMIDST TALL GRASS, 1880. Canvas, 0.60 m. by 0.73 m. Musée du Louvre, Paris. Photo Arch. Phot. d'Art et d'Histoire.
LANDSCAPE. 0.105 m. by 0.245 m. Photo Durand-Ruel.

125. A MOSQUE AT ALGIERS, 1882. Private collection. Photo Durand-Ruel.
ON THE TERRACE. A detail. 0.46 m. by 0.55 m. Private collection. Photo Durand-Ruel.

126. A WOMAN READING, 1891. Canvas, 0.42 m. by 0.34 m. Private collection. Photo Durand-Ruel.

127. THE SHEPHERD, 1902-1903. Canvas, 0.81 m. by 0.65 m. Bernheim Jeune, Paris. Photo Durand-Ruel.

128. BATHER. Private collection. Photo Druet.

129. THE «GRANDE BAIGNEUSE» WITH CROSSED LEGS. Canvas, 0.92 m. by 0.73 m. J. Laroche, Paris. Photo Hypérion.

130. GETTING UP. Canvas, 0.65 m. by 0.54 m. Private collection. Photo Durand-Ruel.

131. AFTER THE BATH. Canvas, 1.16 m. by 0.89 m. O. Reinhart, Winterthur. Photo Durand-Ruel.

132. BATHER, 1880. Canvas, 0.80 m. by 0.65 m. Musée Rodin, Paris. Photo Bulloz.

133. BATHER DRYING HERSELF. Canvas, 0.92 m. by 0.73 m. Private collection. Photo Durand-Ruel.

134. BATHER STANDING. Canvas, 0.41 m. by 0.32 m. Private collection. Photo Durand-Ruel.

135. BATHER, 1891. Canvas, 0.81 m. by 0.65 m. Durand-Ruel, Paris. Photo Durand-Ruel.

136. AFTER THE BATH. 0.41 m. by 0.32 m. Private collection. Photo Durand-Ruel.

137. THE TOILET. Canvas, 0.41 m. by 0.32 m. Durand-Ruel, Paris. Photo Hypérion.

138. THE TOILET : WOMAN COMBING HER HAIR, 1910. Canvas, 0.55 m. by 0.46 m. Musée du Louvre, Paris. Photo Durand-Ruel.

139. WOMAN DRESSING HER HAIR, circa 1890. Canvas, 0.65 m. by 0.54 m. Private collection. Photo Durand-Ruel.

140. NUDE WOMAN RECLINING. 0.40 m. by 0.53 m. Durand-Ruel, Paris. Photo Durand-Ruel.
BATHER WITH STUDY OF DRAPERIES, 1883. Drawing.

141. BATHER. Canvas, 0.55 m. by 0.46 m. Private collection, U.S.A. Photo Durand-Ruel.
Pen-and-ink drawing of the « BAIGNEUSE LES CHEVEUX DÉNOUÉS », 1881. 0.27 m. by 0.165 m. Private collection. Photo Durand-Ruel.

142. BATHER ASLEEP, circa 1890-1891. 0.45 m. by 0.61 m. Reinhart, Winterthur. Photo Durand-Ruel.
TWO BATHERS DRYING THEIR SHOULDERS, 1885. Drawing, 0.19 m. by 0.30 m. Private collection. Photo Durand-Ruel.

143. WOMAN RECLINING, 1903. 0.67 m. by 1.60 m. Pierre Renoir collection. Photo Durand-Ruel.
BATHER SEATED DRYING HER ARM, 1885. Drawing and water-colour, 0.335 m. by 0.235 m. Private collection. Photo Durand-Ruel.

144. THREE-QUARTER VIEW OF A BATHER. 0.81 m. by 0.65 m. Private collection. Photo Durand-Ruel.

145. GABRIELLE WITH A ROSE, 1872. Canvas, 0.28 m. by 0.25 m. Musée du Louvre, Paris. Photo Hypérion.

146. STUDIES FOR « LES GRANDES BAIGNEUSES ». Private collection. Photo Bernheim Jeune.
BATHERS, 1885. Drawing, 0.86 m. by 0.54 m. A detail. Hugo Perls collection. Photo Durand-Ruel.

147. STUDIES FOR « LES GRANDES BAIGNEUSES », 1883-1885. Blacklead, 0.245 m. by 0.445 m. Laroche collection, Paris. Photo Druet.
STUDIES FOR « LES GRANDES BAIGNEUSES ». Drawing, 0.24 m. by 0.36 m. Photo Durand-Ruel.

148. LILAC, 1878. 0.65 m. by 0.54 m. Beau collection, Paris. Photo Durand-Ruel.

149. GLADIOLI, 1875. 0.73 m. by 0.60 m. Private collection. Photo Durand-Ruel.

150. ROSES IN A VASE, 1917. Canvas, 0.41 m. by 0.33 m. Private collection. Photo Durand-Ruel.

151. ANEMONES. Canvas, 0.59 m. by 0.49 m. Jacques Laroche collection, Paris. Photo P. Rosenberg.

152. A VASE OF FLOWERS, 1900. Canvas, 0.47 m. by 0.55 m. Private collection. Photo Durand-Ruel.

153. CHRYSANTHEMUMS. Canvas, 0.32 m. by 0.41 m. Durand-Ruel, Paris. Photo Hypérion.

154. JAPANESE MEDLARS. 0.29 m. by 0.43 m. Formerly Mlle Adèle Wolde's collection, at St. Magnus, near Bremen. Photo Durand-Ruel.
THREE APPLES. 0.10 m. by 0.18 m. Private collection. Photo Bernheim Jeune.

155. STRAWBERRIES AND SUGAR-BASIN, circa 1905. Hugo Perls collection. Photo Bernheim Jeune.
FLOWERS AND FRUIT. 0.325 m. by 0.41 m. Private collection. Photo Durand-Ruel.

156. MELON AND FRUIT. 0.46 m. by 0.56 m. Durand-Ruel's private collection, Paris. Photo Durand-Ruel.
PINEAPPLE AND STRAWBERRIES. 0.46 m. by 0.55 m. Private collection. Photo Durand-Ruel.

157. PHEASANT, FIELD-DUCK AND THRUSHES, 1902. Canvas, 0.54 m. by 0.65 m. Private collection. Photo Durand-Ruel.
PARTRIDGE AND FRUIT. 0.24 m. by 0.42 m. Durand-Ruel, Paris. Photo Durand-Ruel.

158. SUGAR-BASIN, GLASS AND LEMON, 1906. Canvas, 0.31 m. by 0.44 m. Private collection. Photo Durand-Ruel.

159. A LEMON AND COFFEE-POT, 1912. Canvas, 0.225 by 0.34 m. Formerly Gangnat collection. Photo Durand-Ruel.

160. VENUS TRIUMPHANT, 1914. Bronze. A. Vollard, Paris. Photo Hypérion.

CONTENTS

PRINTED IN BELGIUM